# Coping with
# Depression

## A Guide to What Works for Patients, Carers, and Professionals

*Dr Costas Papageorgiou*
*Dr Hannah Goring*
*Dr Justin Haslam*

ONEWORLD

OXFORD

COPING WITH DEPRESSION

Published by Oneworld Publications 2011
Reprinted in 2012

Copyright © Costas Papageorgiou, Hannah Goring and Justin Haslam 2011

All rights reserved
Copyright under Berne Convention
A CIP record for this title is available
from the British Library

ISBN 13: 978–1–85168–835–7

Typeset by Jayvee, Trivandrum, India
Cover design by vaguelymemorable.com
Printed and bound by Nørhaven, Denmark

Oneworld Publications
185 Banbury Road
Oxford OX2 7AR
England

Learn more about Oneworld. Join our mailing list to
find out about our latest titles and special offers at:

www.oneworld-publications.com

# Contents

# Acknowledgements

We are especially grateful to all of our patients who we have worked with over the years. They give our work its value and sense of worth, and give us the satisfaction of being able to help.

We would also like to thank Professor Steven Jones, editor of the *Coping With* series, for inviting us to write this book and Juliet Mabey and Fiona Slater at Oneworld Publications for their help and support during all the stages of manuscript preparation.

Dr Costas Papageorgiou – I am very grateful to my wife, Louise, my children Sofia, Eleni and Lucas, and my parents, for giving me the best tools for creating happiness in my life, and for their patience and encouragement during the preparation of this book. I would also like to thank Sue Thorgaard for her manuscript assistance.

Dr Hannah Goring – I would like to thank Anne Hook and Matt Kemsley for feedback on the manuscript, and I would also like to thank my parents and friends for their support in writing my chapters.

Dr Justin Haslam – Thank you to my wife Angela for her unstinting support and tolerance, to Julius and Lydia for enriching my life, and to Costas for believing I could ever apply myself to the task of summarizing my craft in this way.

# Series Foreword

This series is intended to provide clear, accessible and practical information to individuals with a wide range of psychological disorders, as well as to their friends, relatives and interested professionals. As the causes of emotional distress can be complex, books in this series are not designed purely to detail self-treatment information. Instead, each volume sets out to offer guidance on the relevant, evidence-based psychological approaches that are available for the particular condition under discussion. Where appropriate, suggestions are also given on how to apply particular aspects of those techniques that can be incorporated into self-help approaches. Equally important, readers are offered information on which forms of therapy are likely to be beneficial, enabling sufferers to make informed decisions about treatment options with their referring clinician.

Each book also considers aspects of the disorder that are likely to be relevant to each individual's experience of receiving treatment, including the therapeutic approaches of medical professionals, the nature of diagnosis and the myths that might surround a particular disorder. General issues that can also affect a sufferer's quality of life, such as stigma, isolation, self-care and relationships, are also covered in many of the volumes.

The books in this series are not intended to replace thera-pists, since many individuals will need a personal treatment programme from a qualified clinician. However, each title offers individually tailored strategies, devised by highly experi-enced practising clinicians, predominantly based on the latest techniques of cognitive behavioural therapy, which have been shown to be extremely effective in changing the way sufferers think about themselves and their problems. In addition, titles also include a variety of practical features such as rating scales and diary sheets, helpful case studies drawn from real life and a wide range of up-to-date resources including self-help groups, recommended reading and useful websites. Consequently, each book provides the necessary materials for sufferers to become active participants in their own care, enabling con-structive engagement with clinical professionals when needed and, when appropriate, enabling them to take independent action.

Dr Steven Jones
Series Editor

# An introduction to this guide

Depression is one of the most common and disabling mental health problems and psychiatric disorders. It can affect women and men. Depression can occur across all countries, levels of education and employment, and among the famous, rich, poor and people of all races and ethnic backgrounds. As well as the considerable suffering it causes to the individual concerned, depression can have negative consequences on work, family life and relationships. By far the most serious possible consequence of depression is suicide. However, there is good news. Despite its characteristics and consequences, *depression can be treated effectively* and individuals can stop suffering from it. People can recover from depression and seeking help or treatment for it is not a sign of defeat, failure or weakness. It is a first step in getting better.

Whether treatment for depression is sought through public or private health services, what is really important is that such treatment is widely recognized to be effective and delivered by appropriately trained, qualified and experienced professionals. In England and Wales, the National Institute for Health and Clinical Excellence (NICE) was established as 'an independent organization responsible for providing national guidance on promoting good health and preventing and treating ill health' for all healthcare professionals. Clinical guidelines are recommendations for good practice. The guidelines produced by NICE are prepared by groups of healthcare professionals, patients, carers and their representatives, and scientists. The groups examine scientific evidence available on the best way of treating a condition, such as depression, and make specific recommendations based on this evidence. As specialist depression clinicians and researchers, we believe that the better informed patients, their carers and healthcare professionals are about what treatments work best for depression, the better the chances of overcoming this devastating problem.

Based on the NICE guidelines for the treatment of depression, an overall aim of this book is to describe the most essential facts about depression and help readers learn how to overcome it. Although there are numerous published books on the subject of depression, in writing this book we have attempted to provide several unique features. In particular, a key aim of this book is to provide a clear, user-friendly, multi-professional (clinical psychologists and psychiatrist) and jargon-free overview of currently recommended effective, as opposed to speculative or experimental, treatments for depression in one book rather than just having several separate books dedicated to single treatments. We believe that this is very important, as there is no one treatment that is effective for all patients or all types of depression. If one particular treatment does not appear to work for an individual after a period of time, it is important for them to know that there are other effective treatments available. Therefore, individuals need to know what these effective treatments are and what they should expect from them, so that they are able to make informed decisions about the best way to cope with and overcome depression.

In this book, we endeavour to provide helpful information on what treatments work best for people who might be suffering from depression, or who have done so in the past, as well as their relatives, friends, carers and anyone else who is interested in learning about this common problem. Another key feature of this book is that it provides several examples and case histories of individuals with depression who were able to overcome their problems using treatments described in the book, and it includes a complete and unedited chapter written by an individual who suffered from depression. However, this book is not intended to replace professional help from a psychiatrist, clinical psychologist, therapist or doctor, or to provide comprehensive self-help guides for individual treatments. It is specifically intended to encourage people to take an active part in understanding their depression and in helping themselves to cope with and recover from it by using effective methods that have been scientifically proven and found to help people overcome their depression. Another key goal of this book is not only to focus on helping individuals feel well, but also stay well.

Following this brief introduction, the book proceeds with a chapter written by a patient who suffered from recurrent episodes of depression over a number of years and was able to benefit considerably from both pharmacological and psychological treatments. This is a helpful chapter detailing a person's unique experiences of depression and its treatment. If you, or someone you care about, is currently suffering from depression or have had previous episodes of depression, we would encourage you to read chapter 1 to start with because this chapter provides hope, inspiration and motivation through a patient's journey in and out of depression. Chapter 2 provides descriptions of the nature and experience of depression, its diagnosis, the different types of depression, depression and other mental health problems, and a brief and simple questionnaire designed to help you check whether you could be suffering from depression. The next chapter covers some essential facts about depression, such as how common it is, who can be affected by it, the typical course of depression and the effect it can have on people's lives. Chapters 4 to 8 describe in detail how you can effectively overcome depression and change how you feel by changing your biology (medication), how you behave (behavioural activation), what you think and your unhelpful assumptions (cognitive therapy), and, as a unique addition to the above treatments, how you relate (interpersonal psychotherapy). The chapters on psychological treatments for depression (chapters 5 to 8) aim to give a flavour of what these therapies involve and some ideas and methods of the strategies and techniques they suggest can help. If you are currently depressed, you might find it helpful to try out some of the strategies and techniques described. Finally, the book ends with chapter 9, which provides specific advice on how to stay well following recovery from an episode of depression, including an overview of recent developments, such as mindfulness-based cognitive therapy, in the prevention of relapse or recurrence of depression. If you have recently recovered from an episode of depression, you might find it helpful to use chapter 9 to help you to stay well. In appendix 5, we have provided details of some relevant and useful addresses, which can help you to find appropriate professional help. We have also provided a further reading section at the end of the book, and for specific chapters, if you are interested in finding out more about a particular topic. We have written this book with the intention that it will be read in sequence, from beginning to end. However, some people prefer to dip into books or go straight to the topic that particularly interests them, and that is fine too.

Dr Costas Papageorgiou
Dr Hannah Goring
Dr Justin Haslam

# 1

# A journey in and out of depression: a patient's perspective

When I became ill with depression a few years ago, I read everything I could lay my hands on as part of my many attempts to get better. In most of the books I read, authors were telling me about their patients, the problems they had and the progress they had made, and occasionally there might be a few quotes from patients themselves. But these people never seemed 'real' to me. Did they actually exist or were they an amalgam of several patients mixed together for the benefit of the book?

What I needed was to read an ordinary person's account of what had happened to them, their experiences of treatment, what worked and what didn't, and how they had got better, but in their own words not somebody else speaking for them. So, when Dr Costas Papageorgiou asked me if I would be interested in writing a chapter for this book from a patient's perspective, I was delighted and saw it as an opportunity to provide something that would have been enormously helpful, comforting and positive to me when I was at my worst. What I haven't written about here are the signs and symptoms of depression as this is covered comprehensively in chapters 2 and 3 of this book. I have written about my unique and individual experiences of depression, which, of course, may be different for other people. So, here it is, the story of my depression and my recovery in my own words.

## Becoming ill

I was in my early 40s when I was first diagnosed with depression. It took my general practitioner (GP) some considerable time to convince me of this. I had been seeing him with all sorts of ailments for a couple of years, such as irritable bowel syndrome, stomach problems, headaches, lethargy, insomnia and so on. He had checked out everything and could find nothing physically wrong with me.

The problem was that I didn't want to be somebody with depression. In fact, I couldn't be somebody with depression. I had a nice life, a happy marriage and a very successful career. People with depression didn't 'look' like me. They were 'weak' and 'unable to cope'. Not me at all, quite the opposite in fact.

As all other explanations for the way I was feeling were ruled out, I reluctantly had to accept that my GP might be right and I started taking Prozac. It worked well for me. Within four to six weeks I was feeling massively better and after about nine months I came off the medication.

Now and again, I wondered why I had had depression. There were several stressful things going on in my life at the time, which I assumed had caused me to be depressed. But I had taken the medication, got over it, it was history and I could now get on with the rest of my life. How wrong can you be!

About three years later, I suffered another episode of depression and this one was quite a bit worse than the first. I went to see my GP who prescribed Prozac again. It took a bit longer to work this time and I stayed on it for about eighteen months but

I did get better. Once again, there were a number of stressful things going on in my life to which I could attribute the onset of the depression. But I did wonder how other people managed to cope with these events in their lives without becoming clinically depressed.

By this time, I had discovered the word serotonin and concluded that I was just unlucky, as my body simply didn't produce enough of it – so it was really a physical problem not a mental one. Of course, I felt very comfortable with this explanation because, as I mentioned earlier, I didn't want to be seen as weak and unable to cope. But this serotonin idea enabled me to attach a logical explanation to why I had become depressed.

About three years later, I began to be ill again and this time the symptoms were even more severe. Although I didn't know it at the time (thank goodness!) this was the start of a very long and deep depression. My GP was on sick leave and the locum was determined not to prescribe me anti-depressants but instead told me to try St John's Wort for a few months.

My symptoms became worse and three months later my own GP, to my enormous relief, put me back on Prozac. My relief was short-lived. I waited in vain for the Prozac to kick in and for me to start to feel better. After three months, I went onto a higher dose and after a further three months a higher dose still, but with no effect. I was very poorly by this stage so my GP took me off Prozac and started me on Efexor. I waited for the Efexor to work but it didn't. I was prescribed a higher dose and it still had no effect.

During this time (about two years), my GP also tried other approaches. He arranged for me to see two different counsellors. He sent me to see a psychiatrist who told me that my GP's diagnosis was incorrect, that I wasn't suffering from depression and to stop the medication. This terrified me because if this wasn't depression then what on earth was it that was making living so horrendous? Also, although the Efexor wasn't lifting my mood in any way, perhaps it was preventing me from sinking to even worse depths?

In addition to the help from my doctor, I went privately to two other counsellors, I tried reflexology, yoga, meditation, reiki, hypnosis and so many Indian Head Massages it's a wonder I have any hair left! For eight months, I went three times a week on a 120-mile round trip to see an acupuncturist, I brewed and drank three pints of Chinese tea each week and I have lost count of the number of self-help books that I tried. I joined a gym, I did voluntary work, I booked holidays and my diet included every foodstuff known to prompt the production of serotonin. Some things lifted my mood slightly for a brief period, but two years from the onset of this episode of depression I was very ill and unable to function normally in practically every aspect of my life.

The fact that both the medication and everything else I had tried hadn't worked had another effect. I began to believe that I couldn't be helped, that I was incurable. The impact on my depression of knowing that this was as good as I was ever going to be was huge.

I had been suicidal on a number of occasions and now started to stockpile medication. Perversely, at these times I actually began to feel a bit better, perhaps because I had a plan of action and knew, if I had the courage, I could bring an end to the misery.

My GP then referred me to Dr Justin Haslam, a consultant psychiatrist working at the Priory Hospital Altrincham, Cheshire, UK. He had heard good reports about the treatment provided by Dr Haslam, in conjunction with Dr Papageorgiou, a consultant clinical psychologist, for patients with persistent depression. I went to see Dr Haslam but not with a huge amount of optimism. My previous experience with a psychiatrist hadn't been great and after four counsellors the thought of even more 'talking therapy' didn't fill me with enthusiasm either. My lack of confidence was misplaced. Thank goodness I kept that appointment!

## Getting better

I knew, from my first meeting, that this was an approach that was going to help me. It felt as if I had been given a gift. Within a few weeks, I began to improve. Not dramatically or rapidly, but for me any uplift in my mood, however small, was precious. The first thing Dr Haslam did was to change my medication from Efexor to Zispin. As it happens, Zispin was no more effective than the two previous anti-depressants I had been prescribed and after seven weeks it was changed to Dosulepin, which did work. The very fact that Zispin was stopped so quickly made me feel that I was in safe hands, and that there was now a sense of urgency around getting me better. Chapter 4 in this book, which was written by Dr Haslam, provides a very clear and helpful summary of the medical/psychiatric treatment of depression.

In the meantime, I had started work with Dr Papageorgiou and had also agreed to become an inpatient at the hospital. I was hesitant when Dr Haslam first suggested this, partly because it seemed to underline just how ill I was and also because of the stigma attached to being hospitalized for a mental health problem. However, the first concern rather overcame the second and I spent three weeks as an inpatient. There were several benefits to this. Dr Haslam was able to see and monitor me almost daily and make changes to my medication. I was able to see Dr Papageorgiou three times a week and this meant I could immerse myself in the treatment and begin to make real progress.

My psychological treatment with Dr Papageorgiou is what turned my life around. This therapeutic work, which involved behavioural and cognitive therapies, is described in chapters 5,

6 and 7 in this book. This is my interpretation of what he explained to me about the cause of my type of depression. Childhood experiences create beliefs that individuals have about themselves, their world and their future, which they carry through life. Depending on what the experiences were, some of these beliefs can be negative, damaging and self-destructive. During life, events occur which continually bring to the surface these distorted beliefs that individuals have about themselves. Distorted beliefs trigger distorted thoughts, which in turn trigger negative emotional responses and you feel sad, angry, anxious etc. When you feel bad about yourself, you generate more negative thoughts, which in turn produce more negative emotions. There you are, stuck on this mental Ferris wheel and unable to get off.

At every session in the early days, Dr Papageorgiou reminded me of this link between negative thoughts leading to negative emotions. Once he had established in me an understanding and acceptance of this process we moved on to the next part, which was to give me a way of challenging these negative thoughts and replacing them with more realistic ones. This wasn't a new concept to me. I had read about negative thinking in several of the self-help books I had acquired in the previous two years. My problem was that I couldn't make it work on my own. But with professional help, a structured approach and close monitoring and follow-up I was able to use this tool effectively, and eventually automatically, to control the negative thinking that had become such a destructive force in my life. The process started with me having to write down a situation or event in my current life, which was leading to a negative feeling or emotion. Then, in the next column of a thought diary I had to write down the sort of negative thoughts created in me (useless, failure, for example), which were giving rise to my negative feelings.

I then had to write down all the reasons I could think of to justify this view that I had about myself or about a situation. I

took these numerous sheets of paper to my next therapy session
and we would start on the first one. This required me to come
up with reasons why my negative thought might just not be
true! I can remember looking at Dr Papageorgiou in disbelief
the first time he suggested this to me and saying something
along the lines of 'Well what's the point of that? Of course, it's
true. I've put all the reasons down, and anyway I wouldn't be
feeling like this if it wasn't true would I?' We persevered and bit
by bit I began to recognize that my thinking was distorted and
that there were in fact more reasons that contradicted my negative thinking than supported it.

Another important piece of homework during my early
treatment sessions with Dr Papageorgiou was to keep a detailed
activity diary. The activity diary helped me to become more
active, less pessimistic and less depressed. It enabled me to keep
a good balance between pleasurable or enjoyable activities
and those where I could get a good sense of day-to-day achievement or accomplishment. As I became more competent at
challenging my negative thoughts, I was able to put more balance in my life. I allocated time for work, time for enjoyment,
time for relaxing; and I managed to stop doing things like
watching the television, reading a book and making a list all at
the same time!

I was now able to move on to the next stage of therapy. This
was to identify the particular unhelpful assumptions I held
about myself, which caused the distorted thinking to appear in
the first place. We established the two most damaging and
started work on the first one – feeling in some way defective,
unlovable and worthless. I would never have identified this as
an unhelpful assumption, but as soon as I began to talk and read
about it I recognized myself immediately.

The following few months were spent recognizing the ways
in which this unhelpful assumption shows itself, understanding what had caused it and finding and practising ways to

change it. The journey was not easy. It required a huge emotional commitment, willingness to face some distressing facts and a determination to change behaviour learnt over fifty years. Once we had dealt with the first assumption, we moved quickly on to the next one and began the painful but helpful process all over again. One of the things that kept me going was the absolute conviction that this was the right thing for me. My belief in the process has never wavered. I knew that I was getting better and that life was becoming something to look forward to instead of just getting through.

## What worked for me

Being given an explanation of my illness was a big help to me. Some of the things I learnt were a complete revelation and got rid of many of the naive assumptions I had made. This knowledge helped me understand what I was dealing with. Like many things in life, if you don't understand the cause or nature of the problem it's very difficult to change anything. Once I understood the nature of my depression I found myself able to understand the treatment that was being proposed. It sounded logical and it made sense. This in turn led to a recognition that I was in the care of experts. I now know that counselling was never going to solve my problems; neither were some self-help books. In fact, in my opinion, some self-help books were actually dangerous for me as they unearthed truly difficult memories but gave me no way of dealing with the emotions that surfaced at the same time. My depression was too deep, too resistant to medication and too complex to be resolved using some self-help methods. However, although some self-help materials were not helpful to me, I do not believe that this is necessarily the case for all individuals.

Another factor that helped was having a framework to work within. I always knew what stage I was at in the treatment programme and what was coming next. There was usually some homework to be done before my next session and I knew that if I didn't do it (and I frequently didn't want to) I would make less progress and my recovery would be delayed.

An important part of the therapy is that I have never felt that I was having something done to me. From the outset it was very clear that I had a part to play in my recovery and as I got better I began to feel that I owned more and more of the process. That in turn made me feel more in control of my life and of my future, and with that my confidence started to return.

Being supported and guided by skilled people has made me feel safe and protected. I have been pushed when necessary but held back when appropriate. Some of the most distressing issues I have faced have been dealt with in the latter part of the programme, whereas my natural inclination would have been to go directly to the most difficult problems. It has meant that I have been able to deal with the hardest topics from a position of stability and knowledge and by using the tools I had learnt in the earlier stages of therapy.

## What I learnt about myself

I learnt to look at my life as a whole rather than seeing the depressive episodes as isolated, stand-alone incidents that could be 'cured'. I know that my depressions have been caused by something fundamental in my life, not by specific events. I now understand the link between my childhood and the rest of my life. I knew growing up had been stressful and unhappy but I believed I had left that behind and that my adult life was solely down to me. I can now see what a massive influence it has had on the rest of my life. I recognized that to have any quality of life I needed to confront and acknowledge the emotions I felt as a child and which I had hidden for so long. I learnt that having done this I have to move on and accept responsibility for my own happiness and well-being. I learnt that I am actually a very nice, normal, loving and much loved person.

## Where I am now

I have recovered from the most recent episode of depression, which was about five years ago. I am totally confident that it will be my last (chapter 9 provides a helpful guide on how to stay well after recovering from depression). I do have to watch out for the negative thought cycle returning. When it does, I go back to what I learnt with Dr Papageorgiou and challenge my thinking. I have also learnt to recognize that feeling a bit down on some days does not mean that the depression is returning. It just means I am feeling a bit low, perhaps because something stressful or unhappy is going on in my life. I feel in control of my life in a way that I have never previously experienced. I am more selfish but also more caring. Over the course of a year, I gradually stopped taking medication and have stayed well. I am happy and I really hope that, with the guidance of this book, you or someone you care about will become happy again.

# 2

# What is depression and how can you check if you are depressed?

Most people have an idea of what 'depression' means in everyday language. We talk of feeling depressed or low in mood to describe the sadness and despondency that are a normal and common part of human experience. We might speak of feeling depressed following a disappointment, setback, or the loss of something or someone important to us. At times, however, a person's dip in mood goes beyond such feelings of sadness or despondency into what is sometimes termed 'clinical depression'. This involves not only feelings of despondency or sadness but a whole range of debilitating symptoms which can often be bewildering and frightening to the person experiencing them, as well as to their friends and family. It is depression in this sense that is the topic of this book.

## The experience of depression

What is it like to experience depression? In answering this question it is important to bear in mind that no two people will experience depression in precisely the same way. Box 2.1 illustrates with two case examples some of the ways in which depression can be experienced. It typically involves feeling down, low in mood or fed-up. However, sometimes people describe instead feelings of emptiness or numbness, and for others feelings of irritability may be more apparent. It is common to experience feelings of anxiety or anger along with depression. For some people, depression is marked most by a loss of interest or pleasure in activities they previously found enjoyable. This could involve losing enthusiasm for, or interest in, work, hobbies, sex or previously enjoyed social activities.

### Box 2.1. Case examples of the experience of depression

John, aged fifty-two, has been depressed since being made redundant five months ago. He has struggled to find another job, and has started to feel hopeless about the future. He frequently wakes up at 4am and, unable to go back to sleep, pictures himself losing his house and his wife, even though there is no reason to think that this will really happen. He is often irritable with his family, which he then feels guilty about. He has started to have thoughts that he is worthless and that he has nothing to offer his family. Despite their reassurances that this is not the case, he thinks that they would be better off without him and that he would be better off dead.

Kate is a twenty-three year old woman who started feeling depressed during the final year of a college course. Despite doing well in her course so far, she has become preoccupied by thoughts that she is not doing well enough and that she might fail. She feels guilty, thinking that she is useless and that she has let her parents down. She frequently feels tearful, and has very little energy, tending to go back to bed during the day to rest. She previously enjoyed seeing friends and going to the cinema, but recently has stopped almost all social activities, spending most of her time alone in her room.

As well as affecting mood and leading to loss of interest or pleasure in previously enjoyed activities, depression can affect people in a range of other ways, leading to changes in behaviour, changes in thought processes and physical symptoms. In terms of changes in behaviour, people may be slowed down so that they talk or move noticeably slower than normal, or they may instead appear agitated or restless and unable to relax. They may feel they have no motivation to engage in even the most straightforward activities, and they may withdraw from other people. Changes in thinking include difficulties in concentration, decision-making and memory. In addition, it is common for people with depression to have negative thoughts about themselves, the world and the future. They tend to be self-critical and commonly have feelings of guilt, worthlessness or hopelessness about the future. People with depression can also become preoccupied with thoughts of death or suicide. Physical symptoms include reduced energy levels, disturbed sleep and changes in appetite.

The above description reveals that depression can affect many areas of life. It is important to remember that depression is *not* a sign of character weakness or some kind of moral weakness. Nor is it something that people can simply 'snap out of'.

## How depression is diagnosed

To diagnose depression a doctor, psychiatrist or other mental health professional will use agreed criteria provided by systems for classifying and diagnosing mental health problems.[1,2] These systems are not without their problems and limitations, but we describe them here because they are frequently used to diagnose depression, and they provide useful lists of symptoms. The American Psychiatric Association has published one of these systems, which is called the *Diagnostic and Statistical Manual of*

*Mental Disorders.* (This is currently on a revised version of its fourth edition and is known as the DSM-IV-TR for short. The other system currently in use is the *International Classification of Mental and Behavioural Disorders – Version 10* (ICD-10) published by the World Health Organization). The DSM-IV-TR distinguishes between bipolar disorder, which involves periods of both depression and high mood or mania, and unipolar depression, in which people suffer only from depression, without periods of mania. This book focuses on unipolar depression, of which there are also two main types: major depression and a milder, more chronic form of depression known as dysthymia, both described below.

In order to make a diagnosis, the doctor or other professional will usually interview the person seeking help, and may also ask him or her to complete some questionnaires. The interview will often involve questioning about the symptoms listed below, and may also cover other aspects of the person's life, such as any stresses occurring at work, in relationships or in other areas of life. The doctor or mental health professional may also ask about a person's past and background, including whether they have experienced any episodes of depression in the past, and whether they have any family members who have experienced mental health problems. They may also want to speak to a close relative or carer, although this should be with the permission of the person seeking help.

## Major depression

According to the American Psychiatric Association, for a person to be diagnosed with major depression they must have at least five symptoms from the list of nine symptoms described below. The symptoms must have been present for most of the day, nearly every day for at least two consecutive weeks, and they must include one or both of the first two symptoms (depressed mood or loss of interest or pleasure in activities). In addition, the symptoms must have clearly worsened compared with the person's usual state.

1. *Depressed mood.* This could be described by the person as feeling sad, low or discouraged. Alternatively, many individuals report increased irritability.
2. *Loss of interest or pleasure* in nearly all activities (this is sometimes called anhedonia). For instance, this could involve losing interest in hobbies or no longer enjoying previously enjoyed activities.
3. *Changes in appetite.* This typically involves loss of appetite, although in some cases the opposite can occur and there can be increases in appetite along with cravings for specific foods such as sweets or carbohydrates. These changes in appetite may lead to weight loss or weight gain.
4. *Sleep problems.* Various sleep problems can be a symptom of depression, the most common being insomnia. This can involve waking up during the night and having difficulty falling back to sleep, or waking up early in the morning and being unable to return to sleep (known as early-morning awakening). It could also involve difficulty falling asleep. On the other hand, some people with depression sleep more than normal (hypersomnia) with the extra sleep occurring either during the night or during the day.
5. *Change in psychomotor activity.* The term psychomotor refers to the physical effects of depression on one's muscles or movements. This takes the form of either psychomotor retardation or agitation. Psychomotor agitation could involve feeling restless and unable to sit still, pacing or hand-wringing. Psychomotor retardation could involve being slowed down in terms of speech, thinking or body movements. The agitation or retardation must be severe enough to be noticeable by others.

6. *Decreased energy, tiredness and fatigue.* Tasks may seem to require more energy or effort than normal and everyday tasks may take much longer than usual.
7. *Sense of worthlessness or guilt.* This may involve preoccupation with guilt over relatively minor mistakes, or a sense of responsibility for negative events that were not one's fault. It can also involve a negative view of one's worth that has no foundation in fact.
8. *Difficulties concentrating or making decisions.* This could include difficulties with memory or problems concentrating on tasks.
9. *Thoughts of death or suicide.* This might involve a preoccupation with thoughts of death, or thoughts about committing suicide. This could include specific plans to commit suicide.

In order to count towards a diagnosis of major depression, the symptoms must cause the person significant levels of distress or interfere with their typical social or occupational roles. They must not be the result of a medical condition, substance misuse or bereavement. (Note that when complicated bereavements or grief reactions develop, these can lead to episodes of clinical depression, which require appropriate treatment; see chapter 8 for further discussion.) Major depression can be classified as mild, moderate or severe depending on the number of symptoms present.

### Dysthymia

The term dysthymia is used to refer to a form of depression that is milder but longer lasting than major depression. It must have lasted for at least two years, and as well as depressed mood at least two out of a list of six additional symptoms must also have been present for two years. These are changes in appetite,

changes in sleep, low energy, low self-esteem, poor concentra-
tion/difficulty making decisions and feelings of hopelessness.

## Other types of depression

As noted above, no two people will experience depression in
precisely the same way. The criteria described above reveal that
a person can be diagnosed with depression if they experience
some, or all, of a wide range of symptoms. This means that two
people could both be diagnosed with major depression while
experiencing quite different patterns of symptoms. Different
types of depression have been categorized based on patterns of
symptoms commonly seen together.

Traditionally, depression has been divided into two main
types: endogenous and reactive depression. Endogenous depression was also sometimes referred to as 'biological' depression to
reflect the fact that it was thought to be a disease that arose in the
absence of any stress or other psychological cause. On the other
hand, reactive or 'psychological' depression was thought to arise
as a reaction to stressful life events. However, there is little evidence for different kinds of depression based on whether they
have biological or psychological causes. Indeed, often depression
that appears to arise without any obvious stress or psychological
cause can in fact be linked to an accumulation of relatively minor
stresses, or to difficult experiences earlier in the person's life.
Nevertheless, there do appear to be different types of depression
based on patterns of symptoms that often occur together, or
based on when the person becomes depressed. The American
Psychiatric Association lists the types described below.

### Depression with melancholic features

This is a type of depression marked by a loss of interest in all, or
almost all activities, in which the person's depressed mood does
not lift even when something positive occurs. The person

reports the depressed mood to be qualitatively different from the sadness they experience at other times, and it is often accompanied by excessive feelings of guilt. In addition, a person with this type of depression often experiences early-morning awakening, with the depression worse in the morning. There may also be loss of appetite and signs of agitation or of being slowed down.

### Depression with atypical features

Unlike depression with melancholic features, in 'atypical' depression the person's mood typically brightens in response to positive events. In addition, people with this type of depression tend to have an increased appetite and to sleep much more than normal. They may also describe a feeling of 'leaden paralysis', which is a heavy, weighed-down feeling in the arms and legs. With this type of depression there is often a tendency to be highly sensitive to perceived rejection by others. This sensitivity to rejection persists throughout most of the person's life, even when they are not depressed, and may lead to unpredictable relationships or to a tendency to avoid relationships altogether due to fear of rejection.

### Seasonal depression

Seasonal depression, also known as seasonal affective disorder (SAD) is a form of depression that starts and ends depending on the time of year. The person becomes depressed at the same time of year each year, with the depression lifting at other times of the year. In the northern hemisphere, the most common pattern is for people to become depressed in autumn and winter with the depression lifting in the spring. This form of depression tends to involve low energy, increased sleep, overeating and craving for carbohydrates, and can be treated with 'light therapy', which is repeated exposure to bright light in the morning.

Postpartum depression (PPD)

This refers to an episode of major depression that develops within four weeks after giving birth. It should be distinguished from the 'baby blues', which are milder symptoms of depression experienced by many women after giving birth and that last for only a few days.

Depression with psychotic symptoms

This is a form of severe depression in which the person experiences psychotic symptoms, such as delusions or hallucinations, as well as the usual symptoms of depression. Hallucinations typically involve hearing things that are not there. A delusion is a belief that something is true despite clear evidence that it is not true. Commonly, the hallucinations and delusions are consistent with the depression. For instance, a person might hear voices criticizing them or telling them that they are worthless, or they might have a delusional belief that they are responsible for something that is clearly not their fault (such as a war in another country). These delusions and hallucinations only occur during an episode of depression. When the person has recovered from the depression, their psychotic symptoms disappear as well.

## Depression and other mental health problems

In many cases, people with depression experience other mental health problems at the same time. Indeed, about sixty per cent of people with major depression have at least one other mental health problem, the most common being anxiety. This can take the form of generalized anxiety, panic attacks, social phobia or post-traumatic stress disorder (PTSD; this is a type of anxiety disorder that can develop following traumatic events such as war, natural disasters, or road traffic collisions). The further reading section at the end of this book provides details of self-help books about each of these kinds of anxiety disorders for those wishing to know more about them. Symptoms of anxiety can include feelings of apprehension and tension along with a tendency to worry, as well as a range of physical symptoms such as raised heart beat, shortness of breath, or a churning in the stomach. Many people can have a mixture of both anxiety and depression symptoms at the same time.

Misuse of alcohol or drugs is also common amongst people with depression. In some cases, the misuse of alcohol or other substances can arise as a way of coping with depression, as the alcohol or drugs provide temporary relief. However, in the long term they contribute to the symptoms of depression and make matters worse. In other cases the misuse of alcohol or drugs pre-dates the onset of depression, and sometimes treatment of an addiction to drugs or alcohol can relieve the depression.

Other mental health problems that can be experienced by people with depression include eating disorders such as anorexia nervosa and bulimia nervosa (see further reading section for details of self-help books about eating disorders), and personality disorders, which involve persistent patterns of self-defeating behaviour and attitudes that start early in life.

## Depression questionnaire

So far in this chapter we have described what it is like to experience depression, how it is diagnosed and some of the different types of depression. You probably already have an idea of whether or not you or someone you care about is suffering from depression. However, box 2.2 provides a simple questionnaire designed to help you check whether you could be suffering from depression. This is not intended to enable you to self-diagnose, but to help you consider if you have symptoms of depression. (Note that this depression questionnaire has not been scientifically tested and is not intended to be a tool designed to measure the severity of symptoms of depression.)

## Box 2.2. Depression questionnaire

Thinking about the past month, have you had a period of time lasting at least *two consecutive weeks*, when the following statements applied to you for *most of the day, nearly every day*:

| | | |
|---|---|---|
| 1 | I have felt depressed | YES/NO |
| 2 | I have lost interest in all, or almost all, activities | YES/NO |
| 3 | I have noticed a decrease or increase in my appetite or weight | YES/NO |
| 4 | I have been sleeping less than or more than normal | YES/NO |
| 5 | I have felt agitated or slowed down | YES/NO |
| 6 | I have had less energy than normal | YES/NO |
| 7 | I have felt worthless or guilty | YES/NO |
| 8 | I have had difficulty concentrating or making decisions | YES/NO |
| 9 | I have had thoughts about death or suicide | YES/NO |

To interpret this questionnaire, add up the total number of questions to which you answered 'yes'. If the total is five or more, and you answered 'yes' to either question 1 or question 2 (or both), you may be suffering from depression. If this is the case or if you think you might be suffering from depression it is advisable to seek professional help through your doctor or another healthcare professional. If you answered 'yes' to question 9, and are having thoughts about suicide, it is important to speak to your doctor about this as soon as possible. In addition, appendix 5 at the end of the book includes a number of useful website addresses of organizations that can provide support.

## Key points covered in this chapter

• Depression is a common mental health problem, typically involving low mood or a loss of interest or pleasure in usual activities. It also involves a range of other symptoms including physical symptoms, changes in behaviour and changes in thought processes.
• Different individuals experience depression in different ways.
• Depression is formally diagnosed by doctors, psychiatrists or other mental health professionals using criteria from agreed systems of classification of mental health problems, such as that published by the American Psychiatric Association.
• There are different types of depression, including major depression, dysthymia, melancholic depression, atypical depression, seasonal depression, depression with post-partum onset and psychotic depression.
• It is common for people to experience depression at the same time as other mental health problems, such as anxiety, eating disorders or personality disorders. Problems with alcohol or drug misuse also commonly occur alongside depression.

# 3

# What are the key facts and figures about depression?

In the previous chapter, we described the nature of depression and how it is diagnosed. In this chapter, we provide further information about depression, including how common it is, along with possible explanations for why it is more common in women than in men, the links between depression and particular socio-demographic factors, and the typical course and consequences of depression. We end the chapter with some facts and myths about suicide.

## How common is depression?

Depression is one of the most widespread mental health problems, as revealed by recent large-scale surveys in both the USA[1] and in Europe.[2] In one of these surveys,[2] the researchers interviewed over 21,000 people in six European countries in order to determine the prevalence of mental health problems in the population. They found that major depression (see chapter 2) was the single most common mental health problem, with 12.8

per cent of the people interviewed having experienced it at some point in their lives, and 3.9 per cent having experienced it in the past year.[2] Similarly, a national survey of over 9,000 people in the USA found that 16.2 per cent had experienced major depression at some point during their lives and 6.6 per cent had experienced it in the past twelve months.[1] The results of these surveys suggest that, at any given time, between four and seven people in every hundred will have had experience of major depression within the past year, and between thirteen and sixteen people in every hundred will have suffered from it during their lives. Many more people will have had milder symptoms of depression that do not meet the threshold for major depression, but that nevertheless cause suffering to the person concerned. It is, therefore, a widespread problem and it is important for people with depression to realize that they are not alone. Although this might not provide much comfort while depressed, remember that it is one of the most common mental health problems and that effective treatments are available.

## Men, women and depression

Depression is more common in women than in men, with surveys consistently finding that about twice as many women as men suffer from depression.[1,2] These findings are likely to stem in part from the perception that it is more acceptable for women than for men to experience emotional problems, leading to more women than men reporting feelings of depression. Men may tend to express emotional difficulties differently, for example through drug or alcohol misuse, leading to an under-reporting of the number of men with depression. Nevertheless, the difference in rates of depression in men and women cannot be accounted for entirely by these issues and various theories have been proposed to explain this gender difference in depression.

## Biological differences

One theory is that biological differences between men and women can explain the greater incidence of depression in women. Research has examined the role of female hormones associated with pregnancy, menstrual cycles and the menopause in depression. However, generally speaking, the link between hormones and depression is complex[3] and likely to be affected by other factors such as the levels of stress women experience and how they cope with this, as described below.

## Stress exposure

Instead of focusing on biological differences, stress exposure theories suggest that women experience greater levels of stress than men do and that this explains why depression is more common in women. There have been various suggestions about ways in which women's lives are more stressful.[4,5,6,7] For instance, women are more likely to experience traumatic events, such as physical and sexual abuse than men, and these types of stressful events have been consistently linked to women's higher rates of depression.[4] Furthermore, women may be more likely to experience ongoing negative or stressful life circumstances, such as poverty, single-parenting or caring for ill relatives, which are all associated with depression.[5,6] Finally, women's increased likelihood of depression may be linked to inequality within their relationships which may lead them to have less power or control over important decisions and to have greater workloads than their male counterparts.[7]

## Interpersonal orientation

Another explanation for why more women than men experience depression links it to the suggestion that women are more likely than men to feel strong emotional ties to a wide range of people; in other words they have a greater interpersonal orientation.[8] Because of their larger social networks, there may be a greater chance for women that negative events will happen to people they care about, which in turn may lead to increased vulnerability to depression.[9] In addition, some women may have excessive concern about their relationships with others, leading them to feel too responsible for the quality of the relationships and to fail to express their own needs as a result, leading to depression.[10]

## Coping factors

Although various types of stress have been linked to depression, stress does not lead inevitably to depression in either men or women. The resources and coping skills that a person can make use of will affect how likely they are to become depressed when faced with stressful life circumstances. Women in disadvantaged circumstances may have less access to financial resources or emotional support, which in turn may make them more vulnerable to depression. In addition, the ways in which women typically respond to or try to cope with stress and depression have been said to make matters worse. One theory is that women are more likely to respond to difficulties by focusing on their emotions, and on the possible causes and consequences of their distress in a passive and repetitive manner (a coping strategy known as rumination), which can intensify and prolong the symptoms of depression.[11,12] Men, on the other hand are more likely to distract themselves or take problem solving steps which can help to reduce the length of depression.[11,12] Fortunately, as will be discussed in later chapters, it is possible for both men and women to learn new coping strategies to deal effectively with stress and depression.

## Depression and other socio-demographic factors

As well as differences in the rates of depression in men and women, there are also different rates of depression depending on ethnic or cultural background and social status. In general, higher rates of major depression are found in Western than in Asian nations.[13] However, this may not be because depression is less common in Asian countries but because there are cultural differences in how depression is defined and how symptoms of depression are expressed. For instance, in many non-Western countries depressed people may be more likely to report bodily symptoms rather than describe emotional distress.[13]

Within Western countries there is some evidence that there are higher rates of depression in urban areas than in rural areas,[2] although a recent US survey of depression found no differences in urban and rural areas.[1] There tend to be higher rates of all mental health problems amongst people living in poverty and amongst unemployed people.[2] Unemployment, poverty and lower levels of educational attainment are associated with more severe depression.[1] Finally, there is a link between marital status and depression, with higher rates of depression among people who have never been married and among people who are divorced or widowed than among people who are currently married.[1,2] However, it is likely to be the increased stress or lack of resources associated with particular social and marital circumstances, rather than the circumstances in themselves, which lead to increased risk of depression.

## Causes of depression

The above sections allude to a link between depression and stressful life events or circumstances, raising the question 'What causes depression?' There is no simple answer to this question, and many theories have been put forward regarding the causes of depression. These include theories regarding the role of life stresses and social circumstances, biological factors such as inherited genes that predispose one to depression, as well as psychological factors regarding the role of patterns of thinking and behaving associated with depression. Many of these possible causes can interact with one another. For example, stress that occurs very early in a person's life can affect the development of the brain, possibly leading to a biological vulnerability to depression. In general, it is best to view depression as having multiple causes, rather than a single cause. The relative contributions of biological, social and psychological factors, as well as how these interact, will be different for each individual. Subsequent chapters of this book describe some of the theories of depression along with treatments based on these theories including psychological therapies and anti-depressant medication.

## Course of depression

The term 'course of depression' refers to the trajectory of depression through time, including factors such as when people first become depressed, how long the depression lasts and how likely people are to become depressed again in the future.

### Age of onset

A person can become depressed for the first time at any age. However, it most commonly starts during early adulthood,[14] and there is some evidence that depression is increasing amongst younger people.[1] Generally speaking, the earlier a person first experiences depression the greater his or her chance of experiencing future episodes and other negative consequences, such as difficulty performing their usual roles in work or family life.

## Duration and recurrence

Most people can expect to recover from an episode of major depression within three to six months.[1] However, there is wide variability between individuals in how long they remain depressed, and at least a quarter of people experience chronic depression lasting for two years or longer.[15] In addition, many people who do recover are left with persistent low-level symptoms,[16] and are more likely to go on to have further episodes following their recovery.[17] There is evidence that the more episodes a person has had the greater the risk of future episodes, with subsequent episodes becoming closer together with shorter periods of recovery between them.[18] Fortunately, however, treatments are available for depression that reduce the likelihood of future episodes of depression and provide strategies for dealing with persistent low-level symptoms. The picture is therefore not as gloomy as this research would seem to suggest. Treatments, such as mindfulness-based cognitive therapy, and specific coping strategies, such as problem solving, that can help to reduce vulnerability to future episodes of depression are discussed further in chapter 9.

## Consequences of depression

The negative consequences of depression should not be underestimated. As well as the suffering it causes to the individual concerned it can have negative effects on work, on family life and on marital relationships. These negative consequences generally disappear, however, once the depression has lifted. In terms of effects on work, depression can lead to high rates of absenteeism as well as reduced productivity.[1] Amongst students it is associated with reduced academic attainment and higher rates of dropping out of school or college.[19] Depression can also have a negative impact on parenting,[20] despite the fact that depressed parents typically very much want to be good parents. It is not difficult to appreciate how the low mood, reduced energy and other symptoms of depression can lead to difficulties in engaging in activities such as work, studying or caring for children. In addition, depression can result in marital problems, although it should be remembered that difficulties in relationships, as well as work or family problems, can all contribute to the development of depression in the first place. According to the World Health Organization, depression is one of the leading causes of disability worldwide[21] and the impairments associated with depression have been found to be comparable to those caused by chronic physical disorders such as arthritis, asthma, diabetes and hypertension.

## Suicide

The most serious possible consequence of depression is suicide. As noted in the previous chapter, thoughts about death or suicide are one of the criteria used to diagnose depression. Although this may be an alarming topic for many people, we believe it is important to address it rather than shy away from it. Not everyone with depression will have thoughts of suicide, and it is more common to have thoughts about not wanting to be alive than to attempt or commit suicide. It should be remembered that depression can be successfully treated, and the thoughts of death or suicide will usually disappear once the depression has lifted. It is thought that about half of people who attempt suicide are depressed at the time, although it should be kept in mind that not everyone who attempts or commits suicide is depressed. There are many misconceptions about suicide and some myths and facts about suicide are described below and in box 3.1.[22]

## Box 3.1 Myths and facts about suicide

1. *Myth:* Thinking about suicide is rare.
   *Fact:* Suicidal thoughts are not uncommon and many people, including those who are not depressed, have occasional thoughts about suicide.

2. *Myth:* Only severely depressed people commit suicide.
   *Fact:* Although suicide is linked to depression, many people who take their own lives are not depressed. In fact, in those who are depressed, it is often when their mood starts to improve and they have more energy and motivation that they are most at risk of ending their lives.

3. *Myth:* Asking or talking to people about suicidal thoughts, particularly when they are depressed, could put the idea into their heads and lead them to commit suicide even if it had not occurred to them before.
   *Fact:* Asking a person about suicidal thoughts will not make them commit suicide. It can be a huge relief for people to be given the opportunity to talk about any suicidal thoughts they may be having.

4. *Myth:* People who talk about suicide will not actually commit suicide.
   *Fact:* Most people who take their own lives have talked about suicide beforehand.

5. *Myth:* People who commit suicide do not give any warning about their intentions to end their life.
   *Fact:* As noted above, people who commit suicide usually give many warnings, including talking about their plans.

6. *Myth:* People in particular religious groups will not commit suicide.
   *Fact:* Although some religions prohibit suicide this does not mean that people who are members of these religious groups will not commit suicide.

Adapted from A. D. Pokorny, 1968, 'Myths about suicide'. In H. L. P. Resnik (ed.), *Suicidal Behaviors.* Boston: Little Brown.

Almost half of people who commit suicide have made at least one previous attempt at taking their own life. On the other hand, about two-thirds of people who make one uncompleted attempt never go on to make another attempt. Suicide is almost four times as common in men as in women, although women are more likely than men to attempt suicide but survive. This may be due to the different methods of suicide typically chosen by men and women. Women are more likely to take an overdose of medication such as sleeping tablets. This gives a greater chance of survival than the more violent methods, such as hanging or shooting methods, typically chosen by men. On the other hand, this is not to underestimate the dangers of taking an overdose, which can lead to long-term health complications even if the person survives. People of any age can attempt or commit suicide and there is an increased risk of suicide in people who are divorced or widowed.

Suicide can leave the friends and family of the person who has taken their own life feeling devastated. It can result in long-standing feelings of distress and guilt in those left behind. If you are experiencing suicidal thoughts or are concerned that a friend or relative might be, it is important to seek professional help as soon as possible. All the negative consequences of depression generally disappear entirely when the person recovers from depression, and, fortunately, effective treatments for depression exist. These are described in the rest of this book.

## Key points covered in this chapter

- Depression is one of the most common mental health problems.
- Women are approximately twice as likely as men to experience depression, and various theories have been suggested to explain this, including biological theories, stress exposure

theories and theories about coping factors available to men and women.

- Higher rates of depression have been reported in Westernized industrial nations than in Asian countries.
- Unemployment and poverty are associated with increased levels of depression, as are being widowed, divorced or never married, as opposed to currently married.
- Depression is likely to have multiple causes rather than a single cause, and theories of the causes of depression have focused on potential social, biological and psychological causes.
- Depression can start at any age, but most commonly starts during early adulthood and may be increasing amongst younger people.
- Episodes of depression typically last for three to six months, although they can last for much longer. It is common for people to go on to have more episodes of depression in the future.
- Depression can have negative consequences on work, family life and interpersonal relationships, and it can result in suicide.
- Effective treatments for depression exist, which can reduce the likelihood of future episodes of depression. Following recovery, the negative consequences of depression disappear as well.

# 4

# Changing how you feel by changing your biology: a psychiatrist's perspective

Most of my patients are themselves quite resilient people who are used to solving problems and see themselves as strong individuals. They have often faced and got through serious negative life events in the past without struggling like they are now. They have often battled on for a long time; yet they believe that they are 'weak' to now be seeking help and that they have 'given in'. They are also often surrounded by friends or relatives with similarly robust attitudes to life and have heard all the normal phrases, roughly translated into 'pull yourself together' many times. In fact, they have used these phrases on themselves countless times. Some people criticise themselves for feeling bad and will argue that they 'haven't really got anything to be depressed about'. They may have started to avoid the news, either because it distresses them in itself or because it makes them feel guilty for feeling like they do when 'people out there' have even bigger problems.

Many of the patients I see have been reluctant to consider the option of medication. They want advice on what they can do for themselves. There is a lot they can do to help the process of recovery and a great deal to be gained from psychological treatment, and the issue of whether medication is needed as well should not devalue this. Medication, particularly for severe forms of depression, might just be the most effective way to secure a recovery and the best way to capitalize on psychological interventions too. Taking medication, though, is a passive activity and therefore inherently unsatisfactory to capable individuals. I also think that anti-depressant medication needs a new name, because these drugs also help to treat anxiety disorders such as phobias, obsessive-compulsive disorder and post-traumatic stress disorder. Depression often goes hand in hand with anxiety and both will usually respond to the same treatment. My clinical psychology colleagues and I work together, not apart or against each other, and they at times ask my patients to seek more advice on the potential for their medication to be adjusted or optimized if they can see someone reaching a plateau or struggling.

## Normal sadness versus clinical depression

The key to discussions about treatment of depression using medication hinges on two things: the certainty of the diagnosis and the severity of the depression. This is because clinical depression is a neurobiological disorder, a real illness, which crosses the boundary past normal life sadness and melancholy. However, this issue is much more complicated than that, and beyond the scope of this book, as mild and chronic forms of depression are also viewed as neurobiological disorders. We use the phrase 'clinical depression' because of the absorption of the word depression into common parlance, which devalues it. People talk freely of being 'depressed', meaning by default that this relates to circumstances and is temporary. We react emotionally to life events, but one of the key jobs and expertise of a psychiatrist is to evaluate when this goes beyond normal reactions, and this certainly is not to medicalize normal life and experiences. As discussed in chapter 2, clinical depression is diagnosed when at least five symptoms out of a list of nine have been present for most of the day, nearly every day for at least two consecutive weeks. This is how normal sadness and clinical depression are distinguished.

It might help to make the comparison with high blood pressure (hypertension) for a few reasons. First, it is also a disorder of a regulating system and the medical profession has to decide where the boundary is with normal and illness. Second, with mild or borderline hypertension there is the opportunity for motivated people to make lifestyle changes, which can have an impact. Third, whilst many people can blame 'stress' for their hypertension, it may be only one component of the picture, the symptoms remain and still need treating. Fourth, worse cases have an increasing need to be medicated. Fifth, once stabilized, medication is ongoing. The great relief with clinical depression though is that treatment is not usually indefinite, as it is for hypertension, but the duration of a course of treatment and the different medication options available are very important and this will be discussed later.

## The option of taking medication

Some people may have been offered medication before and refused. This can be for many reasons, but it is sometimes because their GP or family doctor has not, in their eyes, spent enough time with them to explain and justify this path and not make it look like a shortcut, fobbing off exercise or quick-fix that everyone gets. The GP's diagnosis and management plan may be accurate, but seeing a specialist, and being thoroughly assessed, can be much more reassuring for patients as advice will then be seen to be well-founded. The advice involves education, negotiation, and suggestions on further fact-finding to arrive at an informed choice. Another very significant reason to refuse medication is what I call the 'understandability trap', which operates at many different levels in the minds of individuals and even professionals too. Some people will be thinking 'I'm only depressed because ...' and, quite rightly argue that 'medication won't change that', but if you recall the hypertension comparison, the point is that if the illness of depression has been triggered, it needs to be treated.

It is natural for individuals to seek meaning and causes for their struggle. This is very understandable and research does indeed seem to show that adverse life events carry an increased risk of depression. This risk can even last for a long time after the event, leading to an increased likelihood of cumulative risk. Even supposedly positive events carry an increased risk of depression as they can have stressful consequences such as adapting to a new job or moving house. These highly regarded research studies were retrospective, meaning that they looked at patients who were now ill and investigated whether they had a statistically higher chance of adverse life events prior to becoming ill. The assumption in the first place was the same as a layperson's (i.e. 'What external cause might lead to someone developing depression?'). The results of this research are very compelling, but it is important to recognize that adverse life events are not always present. I have met many robust and life-happy people who will proclaim that there is no good reason for them to be depressed, there have not been causative life events and who say that 'This is ridiculous, I feel so guilty feeling like this when there are so many people worse off than me'.

In today's society, the stigma of mental health issues still looms large and I wish we had a more apt phrase to describe it. Just when I start to think the message is becoming more helpful, there is a press release that undermines it. Various brave individuals have broken cover and 'gone public' with their issues. Most recently, Stephen Fry has done a great deal to help understanding of bipolar disorder. Unfortunately, however, this is not necessarily always well taken. When Robbie Williams acknowledged he had had depression and took anti-depressants, the press were scathing, and the headlines were variations on: 'Robbie admits he's addicted to tranquillisers/anti-depressants.' Let's be clear about one thing, anti-depressants are *not* tranquillizers. They do not just treat the symptoms; they alter the underlying neurochemical and physical brain changes in depression. It would have been hugely beneficial for the press to have acknowledged that Robbie Williams is an individual with the world at his feet for whom the reasons for his depression may not be immediately apparent; maybe this could be an illness that can strike anyone. The key point here is that, even though there are still some misconceptions, the stigma of depression and taking medication has lessened over the years and there are many more people now who can understand and support individuals with depression.

I have met many people who believe that, because they can identify life events or life stressors, which they believe are causative, then medication will not work because it cannot change the events or stressors. In today's society, when so many people do have terrible stresses, this argument has even been used by some doctors in my seminars who attribute their patients' depression to their life situation, which they may, somewhat realistically, feel helpless to change. It is important to remember that a range of recommendations can be made for anti-depressant medication, especially for individuals with more severe forms of depression. Also note that, although some medications may be unsafe for people who have particular medical conditions or who want to get pregnant, psychiatrists who specialize in this field are able to offer specific advice on the best (in terms of safety and effectiveness) medication strategies to use to address these issues.

Even when a clinical depression is 'understandable' in its context, it is still treatable and must be treated. In the case of individuals with huge life difficulties, if their depressions were treated effectively, they might be able to face their situation better, make changes, feel more hopeful and try new ideas. I saw this in sharp focus when I worked at a well-known cancer hospital for over three years. I would see people with cancer at the various stages through that journey and, of course, I was not there to treat that illness. I met hugely distressed people who talked to me openly about their problems, their fears, their reactions, and what it was like for them. It was enormously draining sometimes and I still remember some people's stories vividly fourteen years on. People coped in different ways and many struggled to cope. Coping with cancer is still an important field of research. What it taught me was that I could make a huge difference to some people by just helping and allowing them to talk. This could be enormously powerful and showed me the rewards of therapeutic relationships and communication. Even when people have tried medication with little or no benefit, there are numerous options to help find what works best for a given individual.

It may come as no surprise at all to learn that nearly one in three patients diagnosed with cancer can suffer from depression, or that the risk is more than double that in terminal cancer. What may surprise you is that even those depressions are treatable, despite the unchanging physical reality. Some of the most rewarding and dramatically successful work I have ever done has been in the context of cancer care, and many of those patients too told me they were normally the strong ones for everyone else and that 'this shouldn't be happening to me'. There were times then, too, when I had to help these strong people recognize that their depression was beyond 'normal' reactions and an illness in its own right, which could be treated. It was possible on occasions even to see dramatic improvements in terminally ill people close to dying as the anti-depressants began to work. There was a huge reward in seeing someone in the direst of predicaments feel better and it was very emotive to see the benefits of that improvement for the whole family.

If we know that depression affects around one in four individuals in their life span, this must mean that nobody is immune to depression. In fact, many relatively stronger people demand so much of themselves that they raise their personal risk of depression. They do this by taking on huge workloads, having excessively high standards, working long hours, having less leisure time, etc. Most of the people I see have been battling on for longer than they realized, with even more Herculean efforts, getting less and less return at greater cost. They may also recall negative life events they have not coped with as well as they should have done and may think these were also causative rather than symptomatic and harder to deal with because of the slide into illness.

## What happens at your first psychiatric consultation

When I assess someone for the first time, I try to ascertain whether they have crossed the line and entered illness territory rather than having an extreme but normal reaction to adversity, given their story, background, and personality. I would like to make it clear that I do diagnose the absence of a clinical depression, or the presence of a different disorder, if appropriate. Sometimes the situation is complicated by there being more than one diagnosis. If a clinical depression is present, then the most important feature to assess is how severe it is. Severity will affect the type of treatment to be recommended as well as the setting. Apart from our own clinical assessment, we can use rating scales to help give an idea of the severity of depression. There are a number of helpful questionnaires that can be used to assess the severity of a person's depression. It can be useful in the first instance for someone to see in front of them some questions in black and white, which relate to how they are feeling, and it can even be quite upsetting to see their negative thoughts and feelings laid out in front of them. The next thing I usually do is to ask the individual where they think they fall on the scale of mild, moderate and severe according to their scores. Almost everyone I see significantly underestimates the severity of their depression and might reluctantly rate himself or herself as 'moderate' when they are actually well past the cut-off for 'severe'. This often follows through such that they continue to have more empathy for others and believe that their depression is not as bad as that of other people they meet, for instance, in a group-based treatment programme. Following the assessment, I have a range of responses with the most common being:

1. You do not have a clinical depression and it would be inappropriate to prescribe medication. Perhaps you would benefit from psychological treatment.
2. You have a mild depression and medication *might* help but so will lifestyle changes and psychological treatment such as cognitive-behavioural therapy (CBT). You may elect to do both or delay anti-depressant medication depending on response to non-medication approaches.
3. You are moderately depressed and you should consider medication and putting this with CBT and lifestyle changes might give the best result. It is not a must-do but may become necessary particularly if response is lacklustre.
4. You are moderately/severely depressed and you should really take medication, as CBT alone may be a struggle and less effective.

5. You are severely depressed and you must consider medication as without it you are likely to find it difficult to implement and engage in CBT, at least until a response to medication lowers your severity.

## Why can medication be necessary?

This is the crux for me, that depression is a proper medical condition. And, how can this be so? The brain is no longer a black box we cannot access whilst it is working, and imaging technology has come a long way in recent years. The bottom line is that there are significant changes in the structure and function of key areas of the brain. The earliest and most accessible visualization of this is to view depression as a relative lack of serotonin activity (and two other neurotransmitters) with anti-depressants boosting this activity by slowing down the recycling of serotonin back into the synapse (a small gap separating neurons or nerve cells) for re-use. This is now known to be a huge over-simplification as it is more to do with various brain receptors and feedback mechanisms than absolute levels, but does this really matter? To some people it does, and it can be helpful to mention the structure changes I alluded to earlier. There are two key changes in the depressed brain compared to normal ones, which are actually quite striking. The first is that there is a nucleus (a brain structure consisting of a relatively compact cluster of neurons) in the limbic system (the mood and anxiety regulating area), which has shrunk over time, particularly in the slow, insidious onset depressions. Second, the neuronal connections, usually lush, inter-branching and complex have shrivelled to a minimal level, much like a tree in winter rather than summer. What is amazing about treating depression is that this can be reversed, slowly, over time, as recovery is maintained. This is caused by the stimulation of cellular regeneration hormones (chemicals released by cells that affect other cells), a secondary action of anti-depressants. Nucleus volume can be regained and the lush inter-branching is re-established, with the recovery phase occurring as the same system is pushed to work harder before regenerating. To the enquiring mind this leads to the obvious question as to how this degeneration came about, whether it can be prevented, whether more specific treatments will be possible. More research on these areas is ongoing. It is vital to emphasize that this means you cannot make your chemistry different by an effort of will or make nuclei deep in the brain swell up – you have to get professional help, especially if you are suffering from more severe forms of depression, as medication is not indicated for mild depression.

Now, this regeneration phase is also noteworthy for other reasons to do with relapse and duration of treatment. In a nutshell, most people prescribed anti-depressants by GPs stop too early, and therefore more people fall short of full recovery or relapse than should be the case. Some people stop after twelve weeks because they feel normal again but then jeopardize their recovery through lack of knowledge. We know that the neuronal regeneration is slow (we all know that nerves grow slowly) and we have known for many years that stopping anti-depressants too soon can lead to relapse. In the early years, researchers found that there was a reduced risk of relapse if medication was continued for 4–6 months, and more recent and more sophisticated larger research studies show a need to extend this to around nine months of recovery leading to a total of twelve months.[1] This sounds like a long time but it does pay off. This is, in fact, about how long the regeneration process takes. Putting it into figures helps a lot. If you stop at twelve weeks, even if you have done well, the risk of relapse in the following year is almost eighty per cent. If you see through the proper course, the risk for the following year is only ten per cent. This in itself goes some way to help us understand why you might feel you have heard that people can go backwards after stopping medication – they did not see through the course properly. Unfortunately, more severe, longer duration, and repeated episodes of depression seem to lead to a reduced likelihood of full regeneration – we already knew also that 100 per cent recovery is less likely under these circumstances. This is why you should take care to be patient and give yourself every opportunity to fully rebuild before attempting to gradually reduce medication.

The reason all this is so important is that depression is an illness with every potential to become chronic and to recur. How you treat your episode can influence this. Full recovery or remission is our goal, as incomplete recovery tends to increase the risk of relapse, chronic loss of function, dysfunctional alcohol usage and greater hospital contact for other reasons. Successive episodes are often harder to treat, slower to recover from, need more assertive treatment and patients recover less completely. Even if you are reading this and coming round to accepting the medical model of depression as a real illness, you are likely still to have questions or reservations about medication. It always amazes me that even people who have previously blindly taken illicit drugs are suspicious too. Anti-depressants are scrutinized and questioned by patients more than anti-hypertensive medication, for example, and viewed very differently. Even herbal remedies are easier to swallow, figuratively and literally.

## Misgivings about taking medication

There are many, particularly amongst resilient people, who would rather not take medication, for reasons which might include a few of the following (I will try to address them if I have not already done so):

1. 'Will I still be me?' – Yes, you will still be you, but back to how you should be. Your system is being stimulated back towards your normal state.

2. 'Will I be zombified?' – No, this would be disastrous! Some medications can be somewhat sedating, which might even be useful if you cannot sleep or relax but this needs, of course, to be moderate, not zombifying.

3. 'Will I feel flat and uncaring?' – No, this is not a recovery by anyone's definition. Some people do complain that they have felt like this on anti-depressants and it signifies they are taking the wrong one for their system – they need to have it changed.

4. 'I don't want to be reliant on them' – By this people are usually asking more than one thing and it relates to questions 5, 6 and 7. If your blood pressure got back to normal with treatment you would simply think the treatment was effective, wouldn't you?

5. 'How long do I have to take them for?' – This is outlined above, together with the rationale.

6. 'Will I just go back to square one when I stop them?' – No, if you see through the right length of course for you, the chances of this are slim.

7. 'Do people ever end up having to take them long-term?' – This can happen, but not commonly. It seems that some people's systems do not robustly recalibrate and need to be paced by continuing treatment. Most people assume anti-hypertensives are for life to stabilize the system but do not view them as addictive.

8. 'I don't want to just mask the issues' – As the depression improves, the combination of recovery and effective therapy could help you look at problems with better perspective and find ways forward that would not have occurred to your depressed thinking – this not masking.

9. 'I've been told it's awful stopping them' – It should not be so. There can be some common symptoms of stopping, which vary in severity and can be managed – I will expand later.

That's quite an impressive list of reservations. You may even have thought of others. Hopefully you will find them addressed as this chapter unfolds.

## Taking medication: process and expectations

Let us suppose then, that you are seriously considering trying medication. You will want to know what the process is and what to expect. The true keys to treating depression successfully are being methodical and focused on remission or full recovery. Too many people settle for partial recovery, and this is not an acceptable state of affairs with the risks outlined earlier, let alone the ongoing grind of reduced quality of life. Being methodical involves adhering to a plan of action. In medical terms, this is called an algorithm, which is a technical phrase, in essence, for a flow diagram. Some very good and very large research projects have informed the algorithm and it gives us an essential structure to the process. Having a logical algorithm serves four crucial functions: (1) it indicates the types of medication we use initially and the choices later if the individual does not respond on target; (2) it dictates the timing of review appointments and prompts us to ask whether recovery is on target or not; (3) it provokes us to make a decision on what to do if recovery is not on target; and (4) it guides us on the options available at these review points.

As I assess the situation with a patient, there are a few choices to be made. We may be deciding to initiate an anti-depressant and need to choose one. We might also want to treat some of the most troublesome symptoms. Some people might need something to help them sleep. Others might need some relief from their anxiety and agitation. In these circumstances, we sometimes use an anti-depressant with noted sedating or calming effects but in the short term, until the key treatment starts, we might use a hypnotic (sleeping tablet) or anxiolytic (anxiety reducing medication) in addition. These will fall by the wayside as the person gets better but can be very beneficial in the early stages. The modern hypnotics we use are short-acting by design and will mainly be used to help initiate sleep. They might not keep someone asleep through the night, although they might find it a bit easier to drift off again if they wake. If repeated waking remains a big problem, then a more sedating medication might be added, but there may be a risk of residual sedation the next day.

Anxiolytics are a needlessly controversial subject in the UK. The crux of this is that they can be addictive and there are certainly people who have fallen victim to this. The benzodiazepines were definitely over-used in the past and, as with anything, some people are more vulnerable to addiction than others. The response is often to blame the prescribing clinician and, in today's litigious society, who can blame GPs for being reluctant to prescribe them? As a temporary measure, with people who will use them responsibly, they can be invaluable. They might be taken regularly at first but, as progress occurs, they usually drop by the wayside. There have been a couple of other products released over the years, both of which may help anxiety in some people, but, to be honest, the benzodiazepines remain unchallenged. They are only a symptomatic treatment though and should never be used alone without trying to treat the underlying condition. That would be like using painkillers to mask pain without treating the cause.

When it comes to choosing anti-depressants, I have a mental list of the order in which we would normally use them. This is inspired by the algorithm I mentioned earlier, but it is a guide only. There may be reasons to deviate from the guide, depending on the assessment of an individual. This guide puts a structure in place as follows: (1) selective serotonin re-uptake inhibitors (SSRIs), (2) serotonin and noradrenaline re-uptake inhibitors (SNRIs), (3) tri-cyclic anti-depressants (TCAs) and

(4) monoamine oxidase inhibitors (MAOIs). Interestingly, all of them have a clue in their name as to how they work except the TCAs, which refers to the molecular shape. The TCAs, in fact, work in a broad-spectrum way on more than one neurotransmitter, like some of the others. To be fair, even the SSRIs will stimulate other neurotransmitter pathways by indirect actions. The general principles are the same for all, with some differentiating features I will mention as we go along.

## The selective serotonin re-uptake inhibitors (SSRIs)

When it comes to it, the SSRIs are the usual starting point. They can usually be very helpful, although dosage might need adjusting along the way. They can be viewed as a mild introduction to the world of anti-depressants. They include fluoxetine, sertraline, citalopram, escitalopram and paroxetine. Their frequency of use is probably in that approximate order. All except escitalopram are available as generic medications, which means that the patent has expired and unbranded copies are made by a variety of different companies. This means they are cheap, but still effective. I would advise trying to stick to one manufacturer though as there are differences between them. They were released in the early 1990s onwards with huge marketing campaigns behind them, which hinged upon them being, usually, more tolerable than the earlier medications. They are used hugely in primary care, very often to good effect, but sometimes I end up seeing people who have been left to drift in limbo with a poor response. They got as far as a trial of medication but were not monitored properly. If they were under my care, I would know about it and act, but if they have not been on a logical path, the dose might remain the same, the medication might remain the same, and they are left with more hopelessness about their predicament. They might not be informed enough to know that they have been inadequately managed. There is a huge need for specialist and focused pharmacological care to make sure depression is treated effectively.

I usually start people off with a half dose of medication and gradually increase the dose if tolerability is established. This is easy with all of the SSRIs, except fluoxetine, which comes as a 20 mg capsule, which either needs to be dismantled and half discarded or the branded syrup is used to allow easy dose variation. It is hugely important that, after making the momentous decision to try medication, it goes well. The best way to achieve this is to avoid shocking the system by not starting straight off at a full therapeutic dose. Mild side effects may still occur but should be temporary and manageable. There are occasions when people experience an increase in anxiety as they initiate even these mild SSRIs. This is the other reason to initiate at low dosage, as it will be less severe and easier to cope with, especially if the person is pre-warned. This reaction will either be temporary, in which case it will fade and the medication continues, or it will persist and the medication will have to be stopped. This is why I actively encourage my patients to contact me as soon as possible if they have any misgivings about their medication. If people know that there is back-up, they are reassured and do not call without reason. There are some circumstances when a medication has to be changed and it is better to know this sooner than later. Sometimes someone will need a bit of reassurance and encouragement to help them along.

It does not take much brainpower to realize how distressed someone would be if they were not warned that they might get this reaction, had not got access to back-up, and had a severe reaction provoked by going in at too high a dose. At the very least, it could ruin their faith in medication, but more worryingly it might make them feel hopeless about the prospects of recovery. This could then increase the risk of suicidal thoughts and actions. These can, of course, occur anyway in depression, but the loss of hope could be a powerful provocation. I do think this kindling of anxiety/agitation accounts for a great deal of the perceived risk of suicidal thoughts occurring during medication initiation. A prior warning coupled with a good doctor–patient relationship and open lines of communication go a long way to manage it effectively.

The amazing thing about the power of the mind is that a large proportion of people initiated on a placebo under these circumstances would complain of significant side effects. (A placebo is a 'dummy' treatment or a simulated medical intervention that can lead to perceived or actual changes/improvements.) The whole process is anxiety provoking, particularly if it is not how you would have liked to address the problems. Your system goes on red alert, with high vigilance for problems. Manufacturers do clinical trials with volunteers to try to work out what the side effects of a drug are. It is not as easy as you would think because of the frequent placebo side effects, and the answers come from statistical analysis rather than being as obvious as you might imagine.

## Common side effects of SSRIs

For the majority, it is quite a smooth process and many say they have no side effects. The common ones would be queasiness or loss of appetite, temporary tiredness, washed-out feelings or some heightened anxiety. If you experience heightened anxiety, it can put you off greatly, but it should settle quite quickly. Less commonly, people can get a dry mouth, dizziness if they stand up quickly, sinus/nose congestion, sweatiness, and vivid or disturbing dreams. Most side effects are short-lived (3–5 days), but if they persist I tend to encourage people to contact me so that we can discuss whether to change medication if it really does not seem to suit, or persevere if things are settling or minor. Biodiversity, or individual life differences and variation, is an amazing thing and some people will have terrible side effects from usually 'mild medications' and others find a different, supposedly more 'difficult' medication a breeze to take.

It is worth taking time to mention that one of the longer lasting and troublesome side effects of many anti-depressants is a loss of sex drive or sexual function (arousal or orgasmic). Some people are definitely more sensitive to this side effect than others. It may not seem a big issue when you are depressed, but it is a legitimate quality-of-life issue and although someone with moderate problems may not care about it at first, it may become irksome later when their expectations are to be back at normality. It is entirely valid to raise concerns about side effects to your doctor and even if you might think it is somewhat embarrassing or unimportant, the fact that it bothers you makes it of great importance, particularly if getting irritated about it could provoke you to contemplate discontinuing medication. Sometimes, when people are faced with a good response and recovery from the depression, they decide that they are willing to compromise with diminished sexual function for a period whilst they complete the maintenance phase of treatment and then discontinue, but for other people it can be more appropriate to make a change to a different medication that might have a better side effect profile. For this reason, it is important to mention it to try to make your experience of taking medication as trouble-free as possible. We can try to address it and you must not be shy of mentioning it.

## What happens after you start taking medication

In the first two weeks of medication usually very little happens, though there are always exceptions. People commonly do notice a reduction in anxiety and feel a bit less stressed by things. I have been taken aback at times by the occasional very fast response, which seems not to make biological sense. It only happens very rarely, but I want to mention it because I do believe it is a genuine response occurring in some of the most down-to-earth reliable people, via mechanisms we do not understand. Some doctors could view it less positively, even cynically, as a placebo response, which called the diagnosis into question. Although, very occasionally, people respond to a low dose, we usually need to make sure the medication climbs to a treatment threshold. I might advise caution if someone has been hypersensitive in the past to any medication side effects or is worried about the process. As a routine, I see people fairly early, often at two weeks, to check that the medication is tolerable and check for early signs of response. Improvements start quite subtly and may be a briefly better mood, motivation, or realizing a situation has not provoked as strong a reaction as it would have done previously. At the four weeks review, there are sometimes changes more apparent to me than the individual and it is amazing how many people look better in a way it is hard to define, although obvious hints are increased animation and eye movements. It can be enormously helpful if a family member or partner gives feedback too, as they might have noticed things too. Self-care or general motivation might have improved for example, or people begin to isolate less and even pick up a ringing phone they would have previously ignored. I often hear people say, 'I'm a lot more active, getting things done, even if I don't feel a lot better yet.' Some can themselves even remember their surprise at the first positive sounding thought that occurred in the process.

If the process of change has started we can afford to leave the medication alone and wait for more progress to take place. If we are not sure whether things are taking off yet, we need to evaluate the option of increasing medication, for example, and be proactive. A lot of people take the conservative route and want to wait a bit longer, in which case we will adjourn for one or two weeks, but set a further reference point. In truth, both approaches are fine as long as we remain vigilant. The common path that I enjoy seeing is that people report at four weeks that things are definitely on the move and that they have had some good periods, that they are starting to answer the phone or even, on occasion as time progresses, making phone calls and getting back in touch with people. At eight weeks, they then report feeling much more like their normal selves, at quite a decent level, and at twelve weeks they might report that they are starting to feel better than they have done for a very long time. One sign of recovery that I love to hear, which is quite striking, is that people talk about regaining their enjoyment and interest in music. I think that this is quite a poignant and important change. Although pleasure across the board might have been lost and stands to be gained, the appreciation of music involves quite an abstract function and also involves information processing. People often describe that they start to engage with music, not just switch the music on, but they will start to hum or sing along and a really striking sign, I think, is when people talk about the radio going back on in the car. It is then that they realize that they have struggled to process the information load of enjoying and appreciating music as well as being safe on the road and focusing on the driving. Worse than this, people have previously often been lost in their depressive ruminations and that is all that they can hold onto whilst they are driving, not allowing any distraction or activation from the music.

As time goes by, further regular reviews are necessary and at each one there are two decisions we face: (1) is there evidence that progress towards full recovery is on-going? and (2) if there is not, what are we going to do about it? We absolutely have to have this disciplined approach and to keep reviewing progress very regularly. One of the day-to-day difficulties I face is that these strong and robust people I work with will have in the past acclimatized and reconciled themselves to a lower life level and a frequent discussion is trying to get people to rate themselves against an imaginary scale where 10 out of 10 is them at their best. Many people learn to accept that, at best, they have previously settled for 6–7 out of 10 and do sometimes need to be encouraged to aim higher. The path to more substantial recovery can feel quite like a roller-coaster ride and in my mind I visualize it like watching the early pioneers of flight bumping down the runway, lifting and bumping down several times before finally taking off. One problem though is that the variation, which can be high, leads to ongoing feelings of vulnerability, which is quite unpleasant. Some people even feel that the brief glimpses of better times are painful to lose and very frustrating. The path of recovery thus looks like a jagged graph. It would be a huge disservice to underplay the variability some people experience, which can upset them a lot.

If people are stuck halfway up this horrid graph or not going forward, it is important to review the medication options. This is especially where seeing a specialist counts, as we are familiar with effective drugs but also then handling the crucial next step. The most basic next step is to increase the dosage as mentioned earlier, either if response is lacking or slow. A specialist will have a good notion of the minimal therapeutic doses, average and maximum doses for the various anti-depressants, which backs up this process. This will translate into a drive to be proactive and more assertive with medication to get the job properly done. The first strategy, therefore, may be to increase the dose and this is less disruptive than changing agent altogether. The key to a fair trial of an anti-depressant is Decent Drug, Decent Dose and Decent Duration – all the Ds. There are only one or two anti-depressants that seem very ineffective and they are hardly ever prescribed. The dosage part can be addressed in a straightforward manner. The duration aspect is often the hardest criterion to satisfy as, in reality, it is eight weeks. We do not tend to hang about for this length of time in initiation and will often increase the dose at four or six weeks if we feel the need to stimulate progress. All too often I see patients who have tried too many medications at a low dose for short periods before writing them off, to their detriment in terms of recovery and morale.

Sometimes, if it is not looking promising, we might not simply keep increasing dosage, but intervene earlier with a different strategy. If progress needs a helping hand, we might add a booster agent rather than replace the anti-depressant, this is called 'augmentation'. If response is disappointing, we may elect to try another different anti-depressant, which could work differently or map differently to the person's system. We then would return to the logical progression of our algorithm for guidance, depending on individual features in the patient. Apart from the symptomatic treatments mentioned earlier, there are augmenting agents, which are particularly used for the reduction of arousal and anxiety symptoms. They have neurotransmitter actions of their own, which can help the anti-depressants work better as opposed to just acting symptomatically. These include, in particular, a couple of medications called Olanzapine and Seroquel. When using these medications as augmentation agents, I often have to half-jokingly ask the patients not to read the leaflet that comes in the box. There are obvious hazards in reading any leaflet, as they can be alarming. If you read the leaflets in most boxes of tablets then you will find an extremely daunting and worrying list of side effects. It is equally frightening and off-putting if you looked at the leaflet in a box of decongestants, and yet people either do not bother due to the degree of trust in decongestants, or do not bother because they do not believe the side effects will cause them particular problems and are so keen to have a solution to their dreadful congestion. In this case, people might be alarmed to find that these medications are used for the treatment of psychotic illnesses, such as schizophrenia. It has to be stressed that this is at much higher doses than we use for augmentation in all but the most severe cases. I always make sure that I explain this to an individual so that, hopefully, they do not panic and wonder what on earth they have got themselves into or think that they are a lot more ill than they have been previously told. At lower doses, these medications can be excellent at boosting the effectiveness of anti-depressants through their own chemical action, which is synergistic, meaning acting or working together. Some people can get a really useful boost in mood whilst others experience beneficial improvements in sleeping pattern and reduction in anxiety. These two agents, in particular, might be used later on during the course of treatment if an individual has a partial response, or they may be used sooner because of the acute need for extra calming. If an individual is not responding to a particular anti-depressant, then augmentation might include the addition of one of the anti-psychotic medications (see chapter 2), or another anti-depressant, some of which can be synergistic to each other. There are two in particular called mirtazepine and trazodone, which are used most frequently. The realm of augmentation and combination treatment is very much a specialist field, and there are various strategies beyond the scope of this chapter.

## What about Lithium Carbonate?

It is important at this juncture to mention Lithium Carbonate due to the overly negative image it seems to have. If people have heard of Lithium then they have the assumption that this is used in only extremely serious cases or for very sick people. It is, of course, absolutely true to say that it has been used for many years in the treatment of bipolar disorder (manic depression), but its second most common usage is as a treatment for resistant depression. One of the advantages of Lithium Carbonate is that it is a simple salt compound. It is simply Lithium Carbonate rather than the complex molecules of the anti-depressants and, although this is not always the case, it is very frequently associated with a significant lack of side effects and very good tolerability. Adding Lithium to some of the anti-depressants, particularly the older tri-cyclics has been a staple form of treatment for resistant depression for many years with good effectiveness. The difficulty about Lithium is that it has what is called a therapeutic window, meaning that below a certain level in the bloodstream it is not thought to be very effective and above a certain level in the bloodstream it is thought to be ineffective again, or at an even higher level unhelpful and/or toxic.

The process of initiation of Lithium is, therefore, a logistical test and involves regular blood tests to make sure that the level falls within the right range. The therapeutic range quoted by laboratories is quite broad and varies slightly from one laboratory to another, but the consensus view of the experts would be that actually a good going level of approaching 0.8 mmol/L is the best therapeutic level to have. I find that it is usually very beneficial, if not essential, to recruit the patient themselves in the monitoring process, as it takes a degree of determination to make sure the blood tests occur regularly and on time, and that the blood levels are checked and that this information is fed back to me, rather than ticked and filed at the GP's surgery, because if it comes into the bottom of the therapeutic range by a whisker, then no alarm bells will ring, there will be no asterisks on the blood report, and it will be passed off as good enough. Lithium is a very useful agent because it does have some mild anti-depressant action of its own and also acts as a boosting agent for the anti-depressants. Even in people who have supposedly failed to respond to all manner of anti-depressants, the simple combination of going back to basics and using Lithium with a tri-cyclic anti-depressant can bring about a good response.

In very recent times, there was a leading article in one of the international scientific journals raising the question as to why Lithium usage was in decline when the reported evidence of its usefulness and effectiveness is still increasing. It does appear that the principal reasons for this would be the stigma on the one hand of thinking 'this is a serious medication' and also the high level of escalation of 'medicalisation' involved in repeated blood tests and monitoring the blood level for medication. People worry that they can develop a toxic level of Lithium in the bloodstream and can be quite fearful of this and assume that this is the principal reason for monitoring the blood levels. In reality, if somebody is well established on Lithium and has a normal therapeutic level, then it is actually quite difficult to provoke an elevated toxic blood level. I would often say to a patient that if, for example, they were on holiday and developed diarrhoea and dysentery and knew they were becoming dehydrated, then under these circumstances, if they carried on taking the Lithium, there would be a risk that the blood levels would rise to undesirable levels. The answer is, of course, to stop taking the Lithium at these times and avoid the problem.

Lithium is cleared from the body exclusively through kidney function, which means that you pass it out in your urine. In long-term usage, there does appear to be a gradual inhibition of the concentrating powers of the kidneys and this is why, on an ongoing basis, the blood tests are continued to monitor Lithium levels, kidney function, and also thyroid function, as this can be somewhat inhibited by Lithium. This brings us to the relationship between thyroid function and depression. An under-active thyroid can cause a depression, which lifts when the thyroid is treated. Make sure your baseline blood tests are done to check this. Undetected or undetectable thyroid problems can be significant and adding thyroid hormones can cap off or achieve a recovery. Interestingly, the addition of Lithium can sometimes provoke a quick change in thyroid function, which begs the question as to whether there was already an undetectable vulnerability there. If you get into the situation where you have had a good trial of a medication and change is needed, do not give up as these changes have a significant chance of improvement.

## The serotonin and noradrenaline re-uptake inhibitors (SNRIs)

It is not uncommon to change medication. Some 30% of people might not respond optimally to the first anti-depressant and a methodical approach is essential in these circumstances, especially as the individual may be starting to wonder if they are doing the wrong thing. The change, if dose is no longer an issue, needs to offer something new, to map to another combination of receptors and not more of the same. Too often switches are made within a class of anti-depressant and, to be honest, if one SSRI has not worked, another one is not likely to. We sometimes do switch within group, but this is usually to keep the same action but improve tolerability.

The second most common group of anti-depressants are the SNRIs. They have a broader spectrum of neurotransmitter action and often achieve a success if the SSRIs have missed the mark. They are venlafaxine (Efexor), mirtazepine (Zispin) and duloxetine (Cymbalta). They are still branded and correspondingly expensive. Their side effects are very similar to the SSRIs but with a higher frequency of stimulation, especially at higher doses. This can be a therapeutic benefit if motivation and drive improve, but a problem if agitation and sleeplessness result. Zispin is different in more commonly causing sedation than the other two. This can be desirable in agitation or anxiety and this is the principal attraction in some patients. It is handicapped in attractiveness by its propensity to cause weight-gain, though some people escape this entirely. Venlafaxine was for a time tarnished by warnings that it could cause (minimal) blood pressure increases and changes on electrocardiogram (ECG) activity and is still to be used cautiously in those with heart problems. It has been a very successful medication clinically and can really boost recovery. In terms of side effects, it can trigger migraine or headaches in those already prone and some people experience aching joints. The other main issue, usually at the higher doses would be a degree of over-stimulation, which might range from difficulties initiating sleep to agitation. This can be effectively modified by combining the assertive dose of venlafaxine with mirtazepine and this combination is widely used. Reactions to medications can be very individual and some people can experience tiredness and lethargy with venlafaxine. This would tell me that it is not right for you and it can be relieved by a switch to duloxetine, which has a high chance of not giving the sedation in this situation. This can also be the case in reverse, if someone has sedation with duloxetine. Duloxetine has a broader spectrum of action and a different balance of action than venlafaxine. I looked forward to its release in the UK four years ago, as reports from the USA were very positive. However, it is like all the anti-depressants in that for some people it is fantastic, for others only partially effective, and for some, ineffective. The recurring feedback is that it tends to take a full four weeks to start to work but then can lead to steady progress for eight more weeks or so in a steady manner, with less of a roller-coaster feeling than with some others.

## The tri-cyclic anti-depressants (TCAs)

Beyond the SNRIs we look at the tri-cyclic anti-depressants. These have been around for decades and unfairly labelled as 'old-fashioned' as a result. They bring some side effects into play, which are a lot less common in the other medications, such as retention of urine and blood pressure drops on postural change, such as standing up quickly. They can cause sedation and a terrible dry mouth but can be very effective for some people. All anti-depressants, or medications of any kind, can have side effects and tolerability can be helped by gradual introduction. The new medications coming out through the 1990s tended to make claims about better side effect profiles, but this is not true for everyone and, at the end of the day, what you really want is just to find something effective and to get better. All the TCAs can have the propensity to act on the heart rhythm or cause changes on an ECG, but this is only important for a small number of people, such as those with pre-existing heart problems. One TCA, lofepramine, had these side effects refined out but lost its potency in the process and needs to be used at high doses as a result. One unusual TCA is called clomipramine and this stands alone in having a very significant serotonin emphasis. It was found to have specific effectiveness for obsessive-compulsive disorder compared to the others, and discovering this, in part, led to the development of the SSRIs.

## The monoamine oxidase inhibitors (MAOIs)

Beyond the TCAs we may consider the MAOIs, which are much less commonly used because they interact with something in the diet called tyramine. Food and drink high in tyramine (e.g., most aged cheeses such as parmesan, cured meats such as pepperoni, some wines, etc.) can provoke flushing and rises in blood pressure, and thus some restrictions in diet are necessary. They are not very onerous but can be challenging. If these medications are discussed with you, it is likely that your depression has not responded to a variety of treatments and the restrictions might not seem bad. It is very important to take a perspective on the dietary side of things as the key issue is not to avoid tyramine altogether but to avoid high doses. Thus, although many doctors can remember, patients should avoid Chianti. Hung and matured meats and cheeses have risks associated and may need to be avoided, but make sure you read a reasonable summary of the issue. The good news is that MAOIs can really work well even when all else has failed.

## Recovery from depression and maintenance medication

The delight I get from seeing people start to respond and recover from their depression cannot be matched. In my patients, this often involves the thrill of hearing that they are now feeling better than they have done for many years. This is very satisfying and rewarding but, for obvious reasons, it is also tinged with sadness and sometimes those people themselves face thoughts about 'the wasted years'. This can be most poignant when a woman has experienced post-natal depression, which lingers if not properly dealt with. So many of my patients are amazed at the numbers of other people who admit to their own or family experiences of depression when they 'break cover' and start to tell people what they are struggling with. Thankfully, they are also usually amazed by the level of informal support they get from colleagues and formally from employers.

We should look ahead to the end of treatment. At the end of the maintenance phase of treatment, people's attitudes vary, as you would imagine. Most people are keen to begin the process of discontinuing medication. Some people hit the twelve-month mark and are daunted by the idea of introducing the risk of relapse by reducing medication. If someone is under a lot of current pressure and life events, or suffered a long illness, severe illness or long insidious decline, then I would advise them to consider adjourning to the twenty-four-month mark. Most of the rest, though, can do it successfully with support. Having seen what can be done and how good they can be, they will protect this precious recovery and not let themselves decline far before taking action. It is possible to identify an impending slide and respond quickly to quash it.

The key seems to be not to over-invest emotionally in the outcome of the experiment. I try to get people to shift their attitudes towards a position of valuing their health and recovery most of all, whether or not this is associated with medication usage. If we have found a tolerable agent, which does not interfere with life, then this is of course easier to think. Successful outcomes are also associated with a good supportive relationship with another observer who will feed back to the individual their thoughts on change (and are able to do this by agreement of the individual). Discussion is the key and if this supporter queries decline, the individual will either accept it, or disagree and crucially then agree to monitor the situation over a further short period (i.e. one or two weeks) before discussing again. At first, they may think that understandable life or work stresses have triggered a change, for example, but this ongoing heightened awareness allows further evaluation. The central factor to keep in mind is that a return to medication, or a return to a previously higher dose to keep well is not a failure, simply a practical choice. At the end of the day, being well, living well and having a good life are the priceless rewards.

## Final notes on electroconvulsive therapy (ECT) and transcranial magnetic stimulation (TMS)

ECT is another treatment for depression with an 'image' problem. It is only still used in certain cases because it can be effective. ECT is used in very severe depression when lives are at risk or in fully treatment-resistant situations. In these cases, it can certainly save lives and there are many people who are very thankful for its benefits.

ECT involves having a small electric current passed through your brain tissue with the express purpose of causing pulsing brainwaves like those seen in an epileptic fit. Hence the 'electro' and the 'convulsive' terms used. The 'therapy' part of ECT means that it can be helpful and effective. The reason for the use of the electric current is because it is the safest way of inducing the convulsive activity. Other ways were tried and failed due to risk levels. Please be assured that the current is small and measured in millicoulombs.

There are two main accusations levied at ECT. The first is that 'you don't really know how it works' and the second is 'that's what they did in the film *One Flew Over the Cuckoo's Nest* and turned them all into zombies'. In answer, we do know, in fact, that the convulsive electrical activity causes the large-scale release of neurotransmitters and that this then leads to changes in regulation of the neurotransmitter receptors. Second, ECT will make someone tired until lunchtime but not zombified. Memories are harder to lay down and people often do not remember the period of illness and treatment very well. The only time it is undesirable is when someone later subsequently takes risks with their health after being dreadfully ill because they have forgotten the awfulness of it. Memory laying-down and concentration seem to gradually come back over about three months. In recent years, it has become common-place to give the treatment to one side of the brain, the non-dominant side rather than bilaterally. This does seem to reduce confusion and memory problems, but from a clinical perspective, some psychiatrists believe that it does not seem to be quite as effective. Some people report holes in their memory of life events subsequently, particularly what are called autobiographical memories such as birthdays etc., but even after all these years and concerned research, we probably have to acknowledge that the side effects are very variable.

A course of ECT is usually thought of as being twelve treatments, by tradition, though I am not aware of any scientific reason for this. We usually give treatments based on the clinical response and the course for an individual may be shortened. This has to be carefully considered though, as stopping even a little too soon leaves the door open for relapse and restarting treatment can end up in a greater total. Whilst the treatment is carried out, you are asleep and your muscles relaxed with a paralysing agent so that the convulsion does not hurt you. This is why it is called a 'modified fit'. We only want the brain rather than the physical activity. Before this was routinely done the attending staff or the patient might get injured.

The risks involved relate first to the fact that you are having general anaesthetics, which have a risk themselves, and from the temporary rise in blood pressure during the seizure activity. Thus, it is important to have a healthy cardiovascular system. Contraindications would be a history of heart attack or stroke. During the treatment, medications that reduce the ability to have convulsive electrical activity need to be minimized or stopped and this might include diazepam or sleeping medications and certainly any anti-convulsant mood stabilizers. After five or six treatments, progress is usually noticeable, but at first this is on the day after the treatment and then might wane between them. Stopping the ECT comes after sustained progress occurs. Afterwards, medications need to continue and the addition of Lithium might even be discussed as this hard-won progress must be protected and there is a view that Lithium can help to achieve this. There are good sources of information and you would need to ask lots of questions but do not rule it out if it is suggested.

TMS, again, has to be filed in the 'controversy' drawer as it has its believers and non-believers. We think it would be great if it did work but, as with all new treatments, we do not know if it really does work and whom it might work for. The idea is that creating a focused magnetic field, which penetrates the brain tissues, could stimulate those areas and aid recovery. There is no anaesthetic involved. New treatments often get somewhat of a raw deal clinically as we try them out first on people who have not done well with our first choice of treatment. This is true especially with TMS as it has been researched as an alternative to ECT and even in people resistant to ECT. The jury is still out then as to whether it might be a useful addition to our mainstream toolbox. So far, I have only met one patient who had TMS before I met her and, to be fair, she thought that this treatment had been helpful when nothing else had worked.

## Key points covered in this chapter

- Taking medication is not a sign of defeat, failure or character weakness.
- Taking medication, especially for more severe forms of depression, might just be the most effective way to secure a recovery and the best way to capitalize on psychological interventions too.
- Depression often goes hand in hand with anxiety and they both will usually respond to the same drug treatment.
- The key to discussions about treatment of depression using medication hinges on the certainty of the diagnosis and the severity of the depression.
- Advice on medication involves education, negotiation, and suggestions on further fact-finding to arrive at an informed choice.
- The key changes in the depressed brain can be reversed, slowly, over time as recovery is monitored through appropriate medication.
- Full recovery is vital as depression is an illness with every potential to become chronic and recur.
- A logical medication algorithm guides the process of effective anti-depressant medication.
- According to the medication algorithm, the order in which anti-depressants would normally be used is as follows: SSRIs, SNRIs, TCAs, and MAOIs.
- Other medications such as Lithium can be added to some of

the anti-depressants to assist in the treatment of resistant depression.

• Other medical/psychiatric treatments for depression include ECT, which although it has been controversial, benefits have been reported especially in severe, resistant forms of depression.

# 5

# Changing how you feel by changing how you behave

As noted in chapter 2, depression can have a huge impact on our behaviour. The feelings of fatigue and the lack of motivation that are part of depression can make it seem very difficult to perform everyday tasks that were previously easily performed and it can seem preferable to rest. Activities that were previously meaningful or enjoyable may no longer seem to provide any satisfaction or pleasure, leading us to withdraw from these activities and from social situations. In this chapter, we briefly describe behavioural theories of depression, which focus on these changes in behaviour. We then go on to outline some techniques for changing behaviour that have been found to be very helpful in lifting the mood of depressed people and that can also lead to improvements in the physiological aspects of depression such as sleep and appetite.

## Behavioural theories of depression

Behaviour can be defined as 'everything a person does'.[1] This includes not only our outward behaviour but also our inner experiences such as thinking and feeling, which are viewed as types of 'private' behaviour within behavioural theories. A central idea of these theories is that all behaviour is learned, in that the consequences of our behaviour lead us to learn to repeat some behaviours and to stop others. We are likely to repeat a behaviour that leads to a reward, such as feeling good afterwards or receiving food, praise or money for it. The technical name for such rewards is *positive reinforcement*. For instance, if a child is given pocket money as a reward for helping out with the chores, he or she is likely to help out again in the future. On the other hand, if a behaviour leads to an unpleasant consequence (such as someone criticizing us), or simply to the lack of a reward, we are less likely to repeat that behaviour in the future. In America in the 1970s, psychologist Peter Lewinsohn put forward a theory of depression based on these ideas.[2]

A key idea of this theory is that depressed people do not receive enough positive reinforcement from their environment and so activities seem increasingly unrewarding. There may be various reasons for this. Circumstances such as isolation or the loss of a loved one or of a job may mean that there is reduced availability for receiving positive reinforcement. In addition, the person's own behaviour, such as withdrawal, may decrease their opportunity for engaging in rewarding activities. At the same time, the depressed person may experience more negative outcomes, such as unpleasant or distressing events, which may make them even less likely to engage in potentially rewarding activities. This lack of reinforcement is thought to lead the person to engage in less and less activity and to become increasingly passive, and to also result in low mood. It followed from this that therapy should focus on teaching the person to learn how to get more positive reinforcement from their environment. This would then lead their activity levels to increase and their depression to lift.

Also in the 1970s, another American psychologist, Martin Seligman, developed the learned helplessness theory of depression.[3] According to this theory, people who face unpleasant situations over which they have no control may be susceptible to depression. If they continually see that their actions have little effect on their circumstances, they come to expect to have no control over the unpleasant things that happen to them. This results in them becoming passive, withdrawn and depressed, even if their circumstances change so that they could have more control over events.

Although originally developed in the 1970s, there has recently been a resurgence of interest in these behavioural approaches to depression. For many years, there has been more of an emphasis on helping people with depression to change their thinking, with less of a focus on their behaviour *per se*. However, recent research has revealed that therapy focused primarily on changing behaviour can be very effective in treating depression, leading to a renewed interest in this approach. Techniques for changing your behaviour are described in the rest of this chapter. We provide enough detail to allow you to try the techniques for yourself. If you find this approach useful and would like to know more, we also provide a further reading section for the chapter.

## Behavioural activation

A key concept in behavioural approaches to depression is that of the vicious circle, in which some of the behavioural consequences of depression can actually result in you feeling more depressed, leading to more negative consequences and so to a downward spiral of depression. For example, as a result of feelings of depression, you might withdraw from other people and do less and less. However, the less you do, the more depressed you feel and the less you feel like doing anything else. This is not to say that you do less or withdraw from people to deliberately make yourself more depressed. In fact, the opposite is true: you do these things because in the short term they appear to be the best way of coping with depression. When you feel tired and low, resting seems like the right thing to do. However, in depression, resting does not restore your energy levels but instead makes you feel more lethargic.

The best way to break out of this vicious circle of depression is to become more active, and to look at the effect of new behaviours on your mood or sense of accomplishment. This is known as behavioural activation. This approach does not imply that you should simply snap out of depression by acting differently. If it were that easy you would have done so already. However, in this chapter we outline some techniques that you can use to make it easier to start to change your behaviour, by carefully examining your current behaviour and initially making small changes, to see if these have a positive effect on your mood. Many of the techniques described here are based on those covered by Addis and Martell.[4]

## Activity monitoring

The first step in changing how you feel by changing how you behave is to spend some time closely examining your current behaviour and how it affects your mood. This is called activity monitoring. It is important to start with this because it is a way of becoming more aware of habitual behaviour patterns which might contribute to maintaining depressed mood. For much of the time, we operate on automatic pilot, without full awareness of what we are doing and how it affects us. For instance, many of us have a morning routine that is so habitual and automatic that we can go through the whole routine (getting up, getting washed and dressed and so on) with very little awareness of what we are actually doing. Instead our minds are focused on what we need to do in the day ahead, or on remembering past events, or any number of things other than what we are actually doing in the here and now. Operating on automatic pilot is very common and not usually a cause for concern. When we are depressed, however, we can develop habitual and automatic behaviour patterns, which have the unintentional effect of keeping us depressed. Activity monitoring is, therefore, a way of becoming more aware of these behaviour patterns by examining our behaviour and activities in detail and recording them on an activity monitoring chart.

An example of a chart is included in appendix 1. On this chart, there is space to write down your activities for every hour of the day, every day of the week. To use this chart, simply record your activities in the relevant spaces, hour by hour throughout the day. Below are some tips for completing activity monitoring charts.

- If possible, carry the chart around with you and fill it in either at the time or as soon as possible after each activity. If this is not possible, try to complete it at least three times per day, because if you leave it for too long it will become difficult to recall your activities in enough detail.
- Write down a few specific words for each activity. Do not write 'nothing'. Even if you are sitting on the sofa and thinking, that is worth recording as an activity.
- At the same time as you record your activities on the chart, also make a note of your moods by writing one or two words underneath to describe the emotions that you felt at the time. Sometimes people find it difficult to recognize and label their emotions. If this is the case for you, we provide a list of possible emotion words in box 5.1.
- Rate the intensity of each emotion on a scale of 0–100, with 0 being the least intense you ever felt that emotion and 100

being the most intense. Rating emotions in this way is important to begin to make the link between your behaviour and how you feel.

- Don't worry too much about filling the charts in perfectly, but give yourself credit for taking this first step towards changing your behaviour.

It is a good idea to record your activities and moods for at least a week before looking for patterns or links between your behaviours and emotions, as the more information you record, the more useful it will be. After a week of monitoring, examine all your charts, looking for any patterns, such as particular times of the day, situations or activities that were linked with you feeling more depressed, or particular situations or activities that you found enjoyable. Sometimes people can be surprised to find that their mood varies more than they expected, and that although they thought that nothing was enjoyable, in fact some activities provided some enjoyment or pleasure.

When examining the charts, it is also useful to look for any times when your response to feelings of depression actually seemed to make the depression worse. This might help you to identify any vicious circles, in which attempts to escape from emotional pain may help temporarily but make things worse in the long run. To find these vicious circles, look for any times over the past week when you felt particularly depressed. What did you do immediately afterwards? What happened to your mood? If your mood got worse, could this be related to how you responded to feeling depressed? For example, people often try to cope by withdrawing, sleeping or using alcohol or drugs. While these are natural reactions because they can make you feel better in the short run, they may actually make depression worse in the longer term.

## Box 5.1 Types of emotions

We are all born with the potential to experience certain basic emotions, such as happiness, sadness, anger, fear, disgust, guilt and surprise. These basic emotions can serve a purpose; for example, fear can spur us into action to escape from a potentially dangerous situation, while guilt can prevent us from doing things, which might harm others or it can lead us to make amends if we do. Listed below are some words for different emotions. You can use this list to help you to recognize and label your emotions if this is something you find difficult.

| | | | | |
|---|---|---|---|---|
| happy | pleased | joyful | content | glad |
| sad | depressed | upset | low | miserable |
| angry | furious | annoyed | frustrated | irritated |
| guilty | ashamed | humiliated | embarrassed | satisfied |
| surprised | shocked | disgusted | sickened | afraid |
| anxious | terrified | nervous | panicky | relaxed |

## Activity scheduling

Now that you have spent some time monitoring your current activities and making links between your behaviour and mood, the next step is to start making changes in your behaviour and planning new activities. This is called activity scheduling. The goal initially is to make small changes that have a positive impact on your mood, and to build these into your routine. Don't expect to instantly get rid of your depression altogether. To start activity scheduling, you can use the same charts as you used for activity monitoring to plan your daily activities, following the steps below.

- To start with, look over the activity monitoring charts that you filled in over the past week and identify any times or activities that were associated with feeling worse. For example, your charts might reveal that you tend to feel particularly depressed in the mornings, and that this is linked with lying in bed and dwelling on problems.

- Think of alternative activities that you could do at these times. Initially, try to come up with as many as you can, then choose one or two that you are relatively sure you could do. For example, instead of lying in bed, you might plan to get up and read the newspaper while having breakfast.

- Plan when you are going to do these new activities, by writing them on fresh activity sheets for the week ahead. You can use the same charts as you used for activity monitoring, only you fill them in beforehand to plan your day, instead of filling them in as you go along. Perhaps plan to do the new activities on two or three occasions in the week ahead.

- Writing down when you plan to do the new activities on a chart is important because it can help make them seem more achievable and increase your commitment to doing them.

- Try to include a mixture of new activities that give you a sense of pleasure and a sense of achievement. This could include some chores or tasks that you need to do, as well as activities that you find enjoyable or relaxing. For example, you might plan to spend half an hour doing housework, and then reward yourself with some time spent drinking a cup of coffee and reading a book that you enjoy. It is a good idea to include at least one enjoyable or pleasant activity every day. A list of suggestions for pleasant activities is provided in box 5.2.

- After you have planned your new activities, the next step is to actually do them. Try to approach this as a kind of experiment, keeping an open and curious mind, and engage as fully as you can in the new activities, without worrying at this stage whether they are helping you to feel any better. As before, record on a monitoring sheet what you actually do hour by hour, along with your emotions and a rating of their intensity (out of 100).

- After you have tried the new activities on a few occasions, review the charts, and examine your emotion ratings. If they had a positive impact on your mood, you will probably want to continue with them. If not, continue experimenting with different activities to build up a routine that has a positive impact on your mood.

## Box 5.2 Pleasant activities

This list of pleasant activities is intended to give you ideas, but it is not exhaustive so feel free to come up with your own ideas as well.

| | | |
|---|---|---|
| Listen to music | Visit a friend | Have a warm, relaxing bath |
| Read a book or magazine | Cook a meal | Watch a film |
| Go swimming | Write a diary | Watch a good TV programme |
| Telephone a friend | Do some gardening | Spend time with family |
| Go out for a meal | Have a massage | Go out for a walk |
| Spend time on a hobby | Go to the gym | Buy some new clothes |
| Buy your favourite food | Do a puzzle | Do some sport you enjoy |

## Values and goals

If you have difficulty identifying activities to include on your activity schedule, it can be useful to spend some time thinking about your values and goals in life. You can do this by thinking about the areas of life that are important to you and then thinking of specific goals related to these. Areas of life you could think about include family relationships, such as parenting or relationships with other family members, friendships, intimate relationships, work, education, hobbies, spiritual or religious activities, and activities related to physical well-being, such as exercise and diet. For example, you may decide that friendships are important to you but may have withdrawn from friends since becoming depressed. A specific goal could be to plan to contact an old friend.

## Avoidance

Avoidance is any behaviour that involves escaping from or staying away from potentially unpleasant or threatening situations. One of the behavioural consequences of depression can be a tendency to avoid an increasing number of situations. Although understandable given the effects of depression on energy and motivation, this avoidance can make matters worse and result in the vicious circle of depression mentioned earlier in this chapter. You may be wondering why avoidance is a problem. It can, in fact, be a helpful and natural response to unpleasant or threatening situations. For example, it is helpful to avoid situations that might put your safety at risk, such as walking around a dangerous neighbourhood on your own at night. However, avoidance can also be very unhelpful, and it has long been recognized to play an important part in anxiety disorders. Anxiety can lead us to avoid situations that provoke intense feelings of anxiety, even though we may recognize that the degree of anxiety is out of proportion to the situation. However, the more we avoid these anxiety-provoking situations, the more threatening these situations seem and the more anxious we become, resulting in a vicious circle. This is what maintains anxiety problems such as phobias. It is now recognized that avoidance can play a similar role in contributing to depression.[3]

When we are feeling depressed, more and more situations can appear unpleasant. As it is perfectly natural to want to avoid unpleasant situations, this can lead us to avoid them. Unfortunately, though, this can prevent us from taking steps to solve problems that may actually be contributing to our depression, and so make the depression worse in the long term. For example, many of the behaviours that people use to cope with depression, such as withdrawing, sleeping or using alcohol, can be ways of avoiding or escaping from unpleasant emotions or situations. However, although such behaviours may feel right at the time, they do not do anything to improve the situation in the long term. Furthermore, strategies such as using alcohol can actually make matters worse. Therefore, the kind of avoidance that is a problem in depression has been defined as any behaviour that: (1) helps you temporarily escape from difficult situations or feelings, and (2) fails to improve or even worsens your depression in the long run.[3]

Recognizing and working on avoidance can be a crucial part of ending depression. However, avoidance can sometimes be subtle and difficult to recognize, so it is important to start trying to be aware of it. For example, you may have an important letter to write, but feel low or stressed every time you sit down to work on it. You may find yourself getting up, making a cup of tea and turning on the television. This avoidance may make you feel less stressed in the short term but in the long term the letter still needs to be written, adding to your stress or low mood. Avoidance can take a number of different forms, and it is worth looking carefully at what you are avoiding and what you are doing to avoid it.

## Types of avoidance

The more obvious forms of avoidance include staying away from situations which you predict will be unpleasant, anxiety-provoking or stressful. For example, this might involve staying home from work, or avoiding social situations. However, other common forms of avoidance are more subtle and are described below.

- Procrastination can be a form of avoidance. This involves putting off tasks until later, and so avoiding uncomfortable feelings such as stress or boredom, which might be associated with those tasks.
- Some symptoms of depression such as lethargy, fatigue or withdrawing to bed can be ways of avoiding painful emotions.
- Rumination, which is repetitive negative thinking, can be a way of avoiding painful feelings and of avoiding taking action to solve problems.
- Avoidance can also take the form of subtle psychological ways of not feeling. This might involve 'spacing out' or numbing feelings through watching TV or using drugs or alcohol.

As the above list reveals, many avoidance behaviours are ways of avoiding unpleasant or painful emotions such as sadness, anger, anxiety, guilt or embarrassment, and the situations that trigger these. It may seem natural to want to get rid of such painful feelings, and you may be wondering what is wrong with avoiding them. Indeed, society and the media can sometimes give the impression that we should expect to be happy most of the time. However, painful feelings are in fact a normal and natural part of human experience, and our attempts to avoid these emotions do not make them go away but can actually make them worse. For example, avoiding grief and sadness following a bereavement may prevent you from working through the natural grieving process. Similarly, avoiding anxiety and stress may lead to increased stress in the long run as it does not allow you to deal with the source of the stress. Some strategies such as using alcohol or drugs can also make things worse.

Learning to accept and tolerate difficult emotions and feelings is therefore an important part of working on avoidance. You may find that by allowing yourself to fully experience an emotion, it is not as intolerable or overwhelming as you thought it would be. Overcoming avoidance in depression, therefore, involves allowing yourself to experience painful or uncomfortable feelings, while at the same time not allowing these emotions to rule your behaviour. In other words, it involves acting according to particular goals you have in mind, rather than how you feel at a particular moment in time.

Whether or not a particular behaviour is a form of avoidance depends on the context: behaviour that serves as avoidance in one situation may not be avoidance in another. Take the example of watching television. If you are doing this to avoid an unpleasant task, or to numb your feelings, it is avoidance. However, if you choose to watch a favourite television programme because this gives you pleasure, this serves a different function and is entirely appropriate. The important thing is to examine the circumstances and consequences of the behaviour. If the behaviour involves staying away from an uncomfortable situation, but doing so has prevented you from taking steps to improve the situation, it is avoidance.

## Rumination

As noted above, rumination can be an important type of avoidance. Rumination involves spending long periods of time thinking or brooding about problems such as past mistakes or failures, painful feelings or what is wrong with one's life.[5] Although people who ruminate a lot often believe it is helpful and will help them solve problems, actually, rumination can make it more difficult to solve problems.[5, 6] Rumination takes our focus away from an awareness of what is happening around us as we become absorbed in repeatedly reliving past situations or overanalysing problems. It tends to involve thinking about a problem over and over again in a way that does not actually lead one any closer to finding a 'solution'. In this way, it can serve as a form of avoidance as it takes us away from actually tackling the problem or from fully experiencing an appropriate emotion (such as sadness and grief following the end of a relationship or death of a loved one). Much research has revealed that a tendency to respond to low mood with ruminative thinking is linked to depression,[5, 6] and recognizing and dealing with rumination is therefore an important part of recovery from depression.

Rumination tends to happen quite automatically, and can appear difficult to stop.[5] The first step is to recognize when you are ruminating. It can be helpful to mentally label your thinking as 'ruminating' as soon as you become aware that you are brooding or mulling over problems in a repetitive manner that is making you feel worse. As soon as you have recognized that you are doing this, you can then make a choice to change to a different activity, such as one of the pleasant activities listed in box 5.2. Alternatively, the next section contains some suggestions for taking action to solve problems instead of ruminating.

## Overcoming avoidance

Overcoming avoidance involves finding alternative ways of responding to the triggers for the uncomfortable feelings that you automatically seek to avoid. These alternative responses need to involve taking action rather than avoiding. Changing your behaviour in this way is not easy, and it is important to start by taking small steps rather than attempting to tackle everything you have been avoiding at once. It is natural for the reduced motivation, lack of energy and low mood that are part of depression to make it seem difficult to take action rather than avoid, and tasks can appear overwhelming. You may think you need to wait until your motivation returns and you feel better before doing them. However, in actual fact, increased motivation and improved mood often occur *after* you have started taking action, so it helps to commit to take action even though you may be feeling lacking in motivation. On the other hand, it is unhelpful to try to force yourself to do things in a bullying manner, as this will probably end up making you feel worse. Instead, try to encourage yourself, in a supportive and open-minded way, to gradually approach situations and tasks you have been avoiding.

## Breaking tasks down into small steps

One way to help overcome avoidance is to break tasks down into smaller, more manageable steps. One of the effects of depression can be to make it more difficult to plan or organize how to go about accomplishing tasks, with the result that we can be easily overwhelmed. By deliberately thinking through an activity step by step we can make it seem more achievable and this can also help to keep us focused on the task.

If there are a number of things that you have been avoiding, you could start by making a list of all the tasks you need to do but have been putting off. Then number these in order of priority and take the first one, or, if they are all of equal priority, pick one at random. Think through all the steps you would need to take to carry out this task or activity and write these down. Mentally think through each step, predicting any potential problems and how you might overcome these. Then work through these steps one by one, rewarding yourself after you have finished each step. You can then repeat this process for the next task on your list. Beware of a tendency to want to do everything at once. Even if you get as far as the first step of one task that you need to do, or even as far as making the list, you are further along than you were before you started. Box 5.3 gives an example of how to break a task down into small steps.

Box 5.3 Breaking tasks down

> Jack wanted to start a college course, but had been putting off doing anything about this as he was not sure where to start. He decided to think through the steps involved and write them down, in order to get himself started. He wrote down the following steps:
>
> 1. Use the phone directory and/or internet to find out the contact details of local colleges.
> 2. Contact these by phone or email to request course prospectuses.
> 3. Read through the prospectuses to find courses I am interested in doing.
> 4. Check whether I have the necessary qualifications to start these courses.
> 5. Choose the course I am most interested in that I am qualified to do.
> 6. Contact the college to request an application form to apply for this course.
> 7. Complete and send off this application form.
>
> After writing down these steps, Jack visualized himself working through them one by one. He then started with step 1, and ended up starting a course a few months later.

## Self-soothing

So far, we have focused on ways to engage in more activity, and approach tasks or activities rather than avoid them. However, learning to take care of yourself can also be an important part of challenging depression. Often people with depression feel very guilty about leaving chores undone and feel they need to drive themselves to finish everything before allowing themselves to relax. If you recognize yourself in this, it may be important to learn to nurture yourself. Furthermore, we are sometimes faced with problems that cannot be solved, or may simply need to allow ourselves some solace when faced with distressing circumstances. At these times, self-soothing is an important way of taking care of ourselves.

The goal of self-soothing is to provide a sense of calm or comfort rather than avoiding or blocking out emotional pain. Perhaps you need to allow yourself to spend some time crying or to spend a few hours in bed and reading a good book without feeling guilty about it. Other possible ways to self-soothe are to listen to music, take a long bath, or anything else that makes you feel calmer and provides some temporary respite.

## Key points covered in this chapter

- Behavioural theories of depression focus on people's outward behaviour and emphasize the role of changes in behaviour in maintaining depression.
- A key idea of the behavioural approach to depression is that of the vicious circle, in which one's behaviour when depressed contributes to further depression and so to further behavioural changes.
- Behavioural activation is a way of breaking this vicious circle by becoming more active in a gradual step-by-step manner. Activity monitoring and activity scheduling can be used as part of this process.
- Avoidance is behaviour that helps you temporarily escape from difficult situations or feelings, but fails to improve the situation in the long run. Overcoming different forms of avoidance is an important part of behavioural activation.
- You can make tasks that you may have been avoiding more manageable by breaking them down into small steps and tackling these steps one at a time.
- It is important to try to maintain a balance between activities that provide a sense of accomplishment and those that are enjoyable and relaxing. Try to allow time to take care of or nurture yourself, especially if you are faced with difficult problems that cannot be solved.

# 6

# Changing how you feel by changing what you think

In the previous chapter, we outlined behavioural theories of depression and methods of behavioural activation as a way of changing how you feel. Behavioural methods can be very effective in improving one's mood and lifting one out of depression. For many people, however, it is also beneficial to focus on changing the negative thinking that accompanies depression, which is the topic of this chapter. Therapy focused on changing what we think is known as cognitive therapy and is based on cognitive theories of depression. The word 'cognitive' simply means 'relating to thought', while a cognition is a thought or mental process. One of the most widely known types of psychological therapy for depression is cognitive behavioural therapy (CBT), which combines both cognitive and behavioural techniques into an integrated whole. In this chapter, we outline cognitive theories of depression before going on to describe some of the methods used in cognitive therapy to change how you feel by changing what you think. We provide enough detail for you to be able to try some of these techniques for yourself. Many people gain relief by using these strategies independently as a form of self-help. However, other people (like the author of chapter 1 of this book) found it more beneficial to work with a qualified clinical psychologist or healthcare professional.

## Cognitive theories of depression

Cognitive theories of depression are based on the idea that what we think influences our mood. Within this view, it is not events in themselves that lead to emotions such as depression but our interpretations of and thoughts about these events. The following example illustrates this idea. Imagine that you wake up one morning, look out of the window and see that it has snowed during the night, blanketing the roads and countryside in several inches of snow. How might you feel? There are several possibilities. You might feel a surge of excitement and happiness, picturing yourself going sledging or building a snowman with your children. On the other hand, you might start anticipating driving to work, thinking, 'Oh no, I won't be able to drive safely in these conditions. I might skid and crash the car! But I can't stay at home or my boss won't be happy and might sack me! What am I going to do?' In this case you would probably be feeling quite anxious. Or you might instead think, 'Nobody will want to go out in this weather. I won't be able to meet my friends today as we had planned. I was really looking forward to it; it'll probably be a long time before we can arrange to meet up again.' In this case you might feel sad. The point is, the fact that it has snowed does not in itself lead to excitement, anxiety or sadness; it is our interpretations or thoughts about what this means to us that leads to our emotions, as shown in box 6.1 below.

Box 6.1 The link between thoughts and emotions

| Situation | Thought | Emotion |
| --- | --- | --- |
| It has snowed in the night | I'll go sledging with the the children | Excited, happy |
| | I might skid and crash the car | Anxious, scared |
| | I won't be able to meet my friends as planned | Sad |

According to the cognitive theory of emotional problems, thoughts with particular themes will typically lead to certain emotions. For instance, thoughts in which we judge a situation as threatening or dangerous will usually lead to feelings of fear or anxiety, thoughts in which we appraise a situation as unfair will result in angry feelings, and thoughts about loss or failure will typically lead to feelings of sadness or depression. In any given situation, there are usually many possible interpretations or ways of thinking about it. As well as affecting our emotions, how we interpret or appraise a situation will also have an impact on our subsequent behaviour.

## Beck's theory of depression

Perhaps the most widely known cognitive theory of depression was originally developed by Aaron T. Beck in the 1970s.[1,2] This theory links depression to particular thought patterns and to our underlying beliefs, as described below.

### Negative automatic thoughts

According to Beck's theory, when people are depressed they tend to have particular types of thoughts, which maintain their depression. These are typically negative thoughts about oneself, about the world in general and about one's future. For instance, negative thoughts about oneself might include self-critical thoughts such as 'I'm no good at anything' or 'So many bad things have happened to me, it must be my fault.' Negative thoughts about the world involve interpreting ongoing situations in a negative way. For instance, this might involve interpreting interactions with other people negatively, such as thinking that a friend does not like us or want to spend time with us because they cancelled a meeting at the last minute. Negative thoughts about the future might involve expecting that things will not work out as we had hoped, such as thinking 'I'll never get better from this depression' or 'I won't get that job'.

Beck noticed that depressed people often have an ongoing stream of negative thoughts with these themes, which he called negative automatic thoughts. These are automatic in that they seem to pop into our minds out of nowhere, rather than being the product of any deliberate reasoning or effortful thinking and, because they are believable, we tend to accept them as true without question. They are often so habitual that we are barely aware of them. They can take the form of words, mental images or pictures, and they can be about the future or about memories of the past. However, they are unhelpful as they make us feel more depressed, which in turn leads to the occurrence of more negative automatic thoughts, forming a vicious circle and downward spiral of depression. The nature of negative automatic thoughts is summarized in box 6.2, and we describe techniques to help you recognize your negative automatic thoughts later on in this chapter.

## Beliefs and assumptions

The content of our negative automatic thoughts reflects our underlying beliefs or unhelpful assumptions. In a sense, negative automatic thoughts can be viewed as similar to weeds growing above the ground, whereas our beliefs are like the roots

Box 6.2 The nature of negative automatic thoughts

Negative automatic thoughts are:

- *Negative thoughts or images* about yourself (e.g. I'm no good at anything), the world in general (e.g. other people don't like me) or your future (e.g. my life won't turn out the way I want).
- *Automatic* – they seem to pop into your mind out of nowhere.
- *Plausible* – you accept them as true without questioning them.
- *Habitual* – although you can tune into them, you are often not very aware of them because they are so habitual.
- *Unhelpful* – they make you feel worse.

underneath the ground from which these weeds spring.[3] We all have beliefs and assumptions about the world, which help us to make sense of situations, guide our behaviour and influence how we process information. The kinds of experiences that we have, especially during childhood, influence the nature of the beliefs and assumptions that we develop. For example, suppose that a person has generally been treated well by other people throughout childhood and into adult life. He or she might develop the belief that 'people are basically trustworthy'. On the other hand, a person who throughout childhood has been mistreated might hold the belief 'others will hurt me'. These are examples of core beliefs, which are statements about ourselves, others or the world that we tend to accept without question. Assumptions follow on from these core beliefs and take the form of rules that we live by. These tend to be in the form of 'If ... then ...' rules, or 'should' statements, such as 'If I don't stick up for myself, then people will take advantage of me', or 'I should do my best to please other people.' We are often not aware of our beliefs and rules for living, and tend not to question them, but they have a big impact on how we make sense of the world and on our behaviour.

Unfortunately, although we have good reasons for developing particular beliefs and rules, they can make us vulnerable to depression if they are rigid or extreme. For example, the core belief 'I am inadequate' may lead to the rule 'If I am not successful at everything, then I am no good.' This core belief might lie dormant for as long as this person was successful. However, a failure would trigger the core belief about being inadequate, leading to an upsurge of negative automatic thoughts with this theme, resulting in depression. We will have more to say about beliefs and unhelpful assumptions in chapter 7.

### Thinking biases

In a sense, our beliefs and assumptions can be viewed as a kind of filter through which we see the world. Most of us have heard the phrase 'seeing the world through rose-tinted glasses' to describe someone who perhaps has an overly positive and optimistic view of the world. Well, depression can lead a person to see the world through what might be termed *grey*-tinted glasses, giving thought processes a negative bias and maintaining the depression. For example, a person who is depressed is more likely to remember or take in information that is consistent with his or her negative beliefs and ignore any contradictory information. Beck[1, 2] and subsequent writers have listed a number of different ways in which thoughts can be biased when we are depressed. Ten thinking biases (sometimes also called thinking errors or cognitive distortions) described by Burns[4] are listed below. If you can start to recognize and gain insight into when your thinking might be distorted or biased, you have taken an important step in starting to change your thought patterns. One important point to remember is that biases or errors in thinking are not unique to depressed people. All human beings filter information according to their beliefs about the world, and will try to fit information with their pre-existing beliefs. The main point is that, with depression, we are biased to viewing ourselves and the world more negatively, resulting in a vicious circle of depression.

## Types of thinking biases

### Overgeneralization

This refers to a tendency to draw sweeping generalizations based on a single event. For example, failing one test and thinking 'I'm no good at anything.'

### Mental filter

This involves attending to only a certain detail of a situation and ignoring other, perhaps more relevant aspects, so that the whole situation is understood on the basis of this detail. This might involve attending to and noticing only the negative aspects of an experience and ignoring the positive aspects. For example, you might go to a party and focus on the fact that one particular person did not speak to you, but ignore the fact that many other people at the party *did* speak to you.

### All-or-nothing thinking (also called black-and-white thinking or dichotomous reasoning)

This is a tendency to place all experiences or personal qualities into one of two extreme categories, such as success or failure or good or bad, ignoring the 'grey' areas in between. When depressed, people tend to place themselves in the extreme negative category.

### Self-blame (also called personalization)

This refers to a tendency to take responsibility for things that have little or nothing to do with oneself. For example, seeing another person looking cross, and thinking 'I must have done something wrong.'

## Jumping to conclusions

This involves drawing a conclusion on the basis of inadequate evidence, or when there is evidence contradictory to that conclusion. Two types of jumping to conclusions are mind-reading and fortune-telling. Mind-reading involves jumping to conclusions about what other people are thinking. For example, thinking someone doesn't like you because they don't say 'hello'. Fortune-telling involves jumping to conclusions about what is going to happen in the future. For example, thinking 'nothing will help me get better', when you don't know that this is true.

## Magnification and minimization

These involve evaluating the significance of an event in a way that is out of proportion to the actual event. In the case of magnification, the importance of a negative event is exaggerated so that it is perceived as much more significant than is warranted. This is sometimes also called catastrophizing. For example, imagine that you bump another car's bumper while parking your car. If you then thought 'I'm a terrible driver; I could lose my licence because of this', that would be an example of catastrophizing because this reaction is out of proportion to the seriousness of the mistake. In the case of minimization, the significance of an event or quality is dismissed or undervalued. For example a person might minimize his or her good points and magnify imperfections.

## Emotional reasoning

This involves using emotions as a basis for reasoning, as a guide for behaviour or as evidence for the truth. Examples of emotional reasoning are 'I feel useless, and therefore I won't be able to achieve anything' and 'I feel bad, so I must be a bad person'. However, feelings are not the same as facts, and using emotions to guide your actions can stop you feeling better.

### Disqualifying the positive

This involves discounting positive events or experiences. For example, this might involve putting positive experiences down to luck or chance and viewing them as a one-off.

### 'Should' statements

These involve unrealistic and exaggerated expectations for your own performance, often involving statements using the words 'should', 'ought' or 'must' such as 'I *ought* to do this', 'I *shouldn't* have done that' and 'I *must* feel this'. These sorts of statements often lead to feelings of guilt and anger when we fail to live up to these standards.

### Labelling and name-calling

This is an extreme form of overgeneralization, and involves labelling yourself using emotionally loaded language, for example thinking 'I'm an idiot', after making a mistake.

In the rest of this chapter, we describe some of the techniques used within cognitive therapy to tackle the negative thinking associated with depression. These focus on negative automatic thoughts and thinking biases, rather than on the underlying beliefs and unhelpful assumptions described earlier. However, in chapter 7 of this book, we examine the nature of such beliefs and assumptions in much more detail and provide some techniques for changing them.

## Learning to talk back to negative automatic thoughts

In this section, we look at ways of breaking the vicious cycle of negative thinking and depression by learning to talk back to, or challenge, your negative automatic thoughts. You might wish to refer back to the summary of the nature of negative automatic thoughts provided in box 6.2. There are three steps involved in learning to talk back to these thoughts:

1. Learn to recognize negative automatic thoughts when they go through your mind.
2. Start to look objectively at your negative thoughts to see how helpful or valid they are.
3. Practise responding to your negative thoughts with more helpful alternative thoughts.

As we describe each of these steps, we will provide examples from two people who used these techniques in their therapy for depression, Pauline and Colin.

### 1. Recognizing negative automatic thoughts

The first step in addressing the negative thinking in depression is learning to recognize when negative automatic thoughts are going through your mind. You may not always be fully aware of them because they happen so fast, and they may not always be in the form of verbal thoughts but may instead be mental images that flash into your mind, that you barely notice. It therefore takes practice to notice these thoughts and images as they occur. A good starting point is to notice times when your mood changes and you experience strong unpleasant emotions such as sadness, guilt or anger. Strong emotions such as these are a good indication that you are having negative thoughts, and initially it can be easier to spot the change in emotion than to recognize your thoughts. When you notice a change in your mood for the worse, ask yourself, 'As I started to feel bad, sad, anxious, etc., what negative thoughts went through my mind?', and try to recall any thoughts or mental images.

The following are two examples of negative thoughts that people noticed when they were experiencing strong emotions. Pauline had signed up for an evening class in English Literature, but started feeling depressed during her first class. When she paid attention to her thoughts, she realized that she was thinking, 'I'm never going to be able to do all the work for this class. The other people here are much cleverer than me. The teacher must be wondering why I'm here', and it was these thoughts that were linked to her feeling depressed during the class. Colin was on his way to work when he realized that he had left an important report he had been working on at home. He felt a surge of anger and frustration. When he examined his thoughts he noticed that he was thinking 'I'm such an idiot. I'm always making mistakes like this. This is going to ruin my day because I'll have to go back home to get the report and then I'll be late for work.' The more he thought these things, the more frustrated he felt.

Once you have noticed negative thoughts, it is helpful to write them down, and you can use a thought record for this. An example of a thought record is provided in appendix 2. In the first three columns there is space to write the date, time and situation, your emotions and your negative automatic thoughts. The thought records that Pauline and Colin completed are provided as examples. It can be helpful to rate the strength of your emotions as shown in the examples. You can use a scale of 0–100 for this, where a rating of 0 would mean the lowest possible intensity of emotion and 100 would be the highest possible intensity of emotion. When you fill in a thought record, try to write down your thoughts as accurately as possible, although you do not need to write more than a few words for each thought or image. If you find it hard to identify any thoughts or images, it can be helpful to ask yourself questions about the situation in which your mood changed, such as what the situation means to you and for your future, and what it tells you about yourself or how others see you. Write down your answers on the thought record. If it is not possible to complete the thought record at the time that you have the thoughts, try to jot down or make a mental note of the situation and thoughts at the time, and complete the record fully later on. When you come to fill in the record, if it is hard to remember exactly what the thoughts were, it can be helpful to go through the sequence of events in your mind, trying to recall the details of what happened, how you felt and what your thoughts were.

You may find it uncomfortable or upsetting seeing your thoughts written down in black and white. However, it is an important part of learning to recognize them and it can bring a sense of perspective over them. It is the first step in starting to change your thinking.

## 2. Looking objectively at negative automatic thoughts

After you have started to recognize, identify and write down your negative automatic thoughts, the next step is to test out their validity and examine them objectively. When doing this, it is helpful to try to keep an open mind. By definition, negative automatic thoughts are plausible and believable, and until you examine them carefully, they may seem to be self-evidently true. In fact, some aspects of your negative automatic thoughts might turn out to be accurate. But many of them will not, and the goal is to examine them objectively. Asking yourself the following questions will help you to do this:

1. Am I making any thinking errors? (See the list of types of thinking biases listed earlier in this chapter.) For instance:

   - Am I making any sweeping negative statements about myself as a person on the basis of one event?
   - Am I focusing on the negative and ignoring or discounting any positives?

- Am I blaming myself or taking responsibility for some-thing that I had no control over?
- Am I jumping to conclusions about what someone else is thinking or about what might happen in the future?
- Am I thinking in all-or-nothing terms?
- Am I catastrophizing?
- Am I taking feelings for facts?
- Am I making any 'should' statements?
- Am I calling myself names?

2. What is the evidence for and against this thought?

- What objective facts (rather than interpretations or feel-ings) support this thought?
- Is there any evidence that this thought is not true all of the time?

3. What are the advantages and disadvantages of this way of thinking?

- What effect does it have on how I feel?
- What impact does it have on what I do?
- Is there an alternative thought which would be more helpful?

4. What alternative views are there?

- What would I have thought about this before I got depressed?
- What might someone else who I trusted think about this?
- What would I say to a friend or someone I cared about who was in this situation?
- How else could I interpret what happened?

When Pauline examined her thoughts using these questions, she noticed that she was making some thinking errors. For instance, she realized that she was jumping to conclusions when she thought 'The other people here seem much cleverer than me', as she did not really know that this was true. She was mind-reading when she thought 'The teacher must be wondering why I am here' and she was also predicting the future when she thought 'I'm never going to be able to do all the work for this class'. When she looked for evidence for and against these thoughts, she realized that her evidence for them was that some of the other people in the class had answered more questions than she had, and the teacher had complimented their answers, whereas Pauline had not spoken much in the class. She realized that these thoughts were not particularly helpful as they were affecting her mood, leading to depression, and they were also making her consider dropping out of the class, which she did not really want to do.

When Colin examined his thoughts he realized he was labelling himself ('I'm such an idiot'), overgeneralizing ('I'm always making mistakes like this') and catastrophizing and predicting the future ('This is going to ruin my day'). When he looked at the evidence for these thoughts, he realized that in actual fact, this was the first time in two years in his job that he had left anything at home and had to go back for it.

## 3. Responding to negative automatic thoughts

The final step in challenging negative automatic thoughts is learning to respond to them with alternative, more helpful thoughts. Using all of the information and ideas that you gathered in answering the above questions, can you think of an alternative, more balanced response to this situation? This might be a different interpretation of the original situation, or a more balanced view of it, taking into account evidence both for and against your original negative thought. Your response needs to be realistic and believable. It is important, though, to remember that the goal here is not to generate *positive* thoughts, because these can also be biased and distorted. The aim is not to replace each negative thought with a positive thought, but to generate more objective, realistic and helpful perspectives on thoughts and situations. There is space to write down these new, alternative, thoughts in the fifth column of the thought record.

When Pauline came to think of alternative thoughts with which to respond to her negative automatic thoughts, she found it helpful to imagine what she would say to a friend in a similar situation. This led her to write down 'I won't know whether or not I can do it unless I give myself a chance. I can ask the teacher for help if I am finding it difficult.' Colin weighed up the evidence for and against his negative thoughts and wrote down 'This is the first time I've left a report at home since starting this job. One mistake doesn't make me an idiot. It's frustrating to be delayed by having to go back for it but it won't necessarily ruin my whole day.'

After responding to your negative automatic thoughts with alternative thoughts and writing these down on your thought record, you can then evaluate the impact of these new thoughts on your mood, and re-rate your emotions (0–100) in the final column of the thought record. Both Pauline and Colin found that the intensity of their negative emotions had reduced, although these emotions had not disappeared entirely. If your alternative thoughts have no impact on your emotions, it might be helpful to check how realistic or believable your alternative thoughts are, making sure they are a balanced view of the situation based on the evidence. An empty 'positive' thought that you don't really believe is unlikely to have a positive impact on your mood.

As with any new skill, writing down your negative thoughts and identifying alternative thoughts will probably feel awkward and difficult at first, and it will take practice to become comfortable with it. It is important to get into the habit of actually writing down your thoughts, rather than simply trying to respond to them in your head, because writing them down can help bring a sense of perspective over them. However, as you become more practised at recording your thoughts and responding to them in paper, you might find that you start automatically challenging your negative thoughts, and so there may be less need to write them down.

## Common difficulties with challenging negative automatic thoughts

It is common for people to encounter some obstacles in challenging negative automatic thoughts. By their nature these thoughts can be painful, and sometimes people find themselves avoiding recording them because focusing on them can lead to feelings of upset. It may be useful initially to spend only a limited amount of time focusing on thoughts and then distract yourself from them at other times. At the same time, it is worth recognizing that the very fact that they are painful suggests they are playing a role in your depression, and learning to view them objectively is likely to be beneficial. Some thoughts may be particularly distressing, and this can make it difficult to take a step back from them enough to identify any alternative thoughts. One way round this could be to distract yourself for a while and return to it when you are feeling calmer or less upset, as you may then find yourself more able to view the thought or situation objectively.

Another difficulty is related to wanting to complete the thought records perfectly or being afraid of getting it wrong. There is actually no right or wrong answer when you are challenging negative thoughts. What matters is that it is helpful for you and leads to an improvement in your mood. Similarly, try not to criticize yourself for having the negative thoughts in the first place. They are a symptom of depression and the more you practise challenging them, the easier it will get.

A third difficulty is encountered when negative automatic thoughts take the form of questions (such as 'What if it goes wrong?'). It is difficult to challenge a question, and the best way of approaching this situation is to ask yourself if there is a negative prediction or statement underlying the question (such as 'It's going to go wrong'). Predictions can be tested using behavioural experiments as described below.

## Behavioural experiments

Many negative thoughts take the form of predictions about what might happen in the future. For instance, you might be invited to go away for the weekend to visit some friends, and think 'There's no point going, I won't enjoy it', and stay at home because you are convinced that this is true. As described above, you can challenge a negative thought like this by identifying the thinking error (predicting the future) and writing down an alternative thought based on the evidence. In this example, an alternative might be 'As I cannot predict the future, I don't know whether or not I will enjoy this weekend away. However, past experience tells me that, even though I do not feel like going at the moment, if I do go I might enjoy it more than I expect.' However, until you test out your thought in the real world, you cannot know whether your negative thought or the alternative thought is accurate. Unless you actually go to visit your friends for the weekend, there will be no way of knowing for certain whether or not you will enjoy it. This is where action plans or behavioural experiments come in. For instance, in the above example, you could decide to go to take up the invitation to go away for the weekend to test out your predictions, and afterwards evaluate how much you enjoyed it, to see if the facts fitted more with the negative thought or with the alternative thought.

The term 'behavioural experiment' is used to describe this way of testing out your thoughts because in doing this you are acting a bit like a scientist conducting an experiment to test out your predictions. Like a scientist, you don't know in advance what the outcome of your experiment will be. The idea is to approach it with curiosity and a spirit of enquiry. The steps below describe how to plan a behavioural experiment:

1. Identify a negative thought to be tested and write this down.
2. Identify an alternative to this thought and write this down as well.
3. Devise an experiment to test out these thoughts, seeing the two thoughts as two different predictions regarding what might happen. Plan what you will do, where and when you will do it, and what you will be looking out for.
4. Think through any potential problems and how you could deal with them before going ahead with actually doing your behavioural experiment.
5. Record what happened and how this related to the thoughts you were testing. Does this provide any evidence for or against your original thought or the alternative thought? What do the results mean?
6. Plan further behavioural experiments to follow on from the one you have just done.

It helps to make the thoughts you are testing as specific as you can, otherwise it might be difficult to interpret the results of your experiment.

## Using behavioural experiments to become more active

As described in chapter 5, the experience of depression makes it common for people to reduce their levels of activity, cutting themselves off from their usual sources of enjoyment and stimulation, leading to a vicious circle of depression.

This pattern is often accompanied by thoughts such as 'I don't enjoy anything any more' or 'There's no point doing anything. I'll feel better if I stay in bed.' Some of the techniques described in the previous chapter on behavioural approaches can be combined with behavioural experiments to test out such thoughts.

For instance, suppose you have the thought 'I don't enjoy anything any more.' As described earlier in this chapter, you could record this on a thought record, and respond to it with an alternative, more balanced thought such as 'This could be an example of mental filter. Although since being depressed, I don't enjoy things as much as I used to, there might still be some things I enjoy more than others.' You could then decide to do a behavioural experiment to test this out, using the activity chart discussed in the previous chapter (see appendix 1). To do this, you could record your activities hour by hour, over the course of a week, as described in chapter 5, and as you go along rate how much you enjoy each activity out of 100. At the end of the week, look back over your ratings to see whether this evidence fits with your initial thought (that you don't enjoy anything), or with your alternative thought.

It is not uncommon for people to find, as a result of experiments of this kind, that they are getting more enjoyment and satisfaction out of life than they realized before they started paying more attention to their activity levels. However, you may well decide that there is room for more enjoyment and satisfaction in your life, in which case the next example of a behavioural experiment might help. Suppose you are spending a lot of time in bed, and think 'I'm better off staying in bed. I'll feel worse if I try to do anything.' An alternative thought might be 'Staying in bed hasn't helped much with my depression so far. I won't know how I'll feel if I get up and do something until I try it.' You could then carry out a behavioural experiment in which you use an activity sheet to plan potentially enjoyable activities and again rate levels of enjoyment or satisfaction. You could use this to test whether or not it's true that you feel worse if you do something rather than staying in bed.

The focus of this chapter has been standard cognitive therapy for depression as developed by Aaron T. Beck in the 1970s,[1,2] as this is well established as an evidence-based effective treatment for depression. This kind of therapy focuses on changing the content of your thoughts or *what* you think. However, in recent years there have been several new developments in the understanding and treatment of depression within the cognitive therapy field, which as yet do not have the same degree of research evidence supporting them as standard cognitive therapy. Some examples include metacognitive therapy[5] and acceptance and commitment therapy.[6] Some of the most recent developments in our psychological understanding and treatment of depression have focused on changing *how* you think instead of *what* you think, and relate to the process of depressive rumination.[7] A review of this new and important area of research is beyond the scope and goals of this book, as is a description of all the new developments within cognitive therapy. However, key references are provided in the chapter notes for the interested reader. Other more specific developments within the cognitive therapy field, such as mindfulness-based cognitive therapy, for preventing relapse and recurrence of depression are discussed in chapter 9.

## Key points covered in this chapter

- Cognitive theories of depression focus on the role of negative thinking in depression, and view depressed mood as resulting from negative thoughts, or negative interpretations of events.
- Beck's theory is the most widely known cognitive theory of depression and emphasizes the role of negative automatic

thoughts, thinking biases and underlying beliefs in depression.

- Negative automatic thoughts are negative thoughts about oneself, the world or the future. They seem to come into one's mind out of nowhere and are plausible and believable, although they are unhelpful in that they make one feel worse.
- Negative thoughts can contain a number of thinking biases, such as all-or-nothing thinking, jumping to conclusions or disqualifying the positive.
- Cognitive techniques for coping with depression involve learning to talk back to negative automatic thoughts by learning to recognize negative thoughts and thinking biases, and to identify alternative thoughts.
- Behavioural experiments are a way of testing out negative thoughts and alternative thoughts in the real world.

# 7

# Changing how you feel by changing your unhelpful assumptions

In chapter 6, we saw that the cognitive therapy method of identifying and challenging negative automatic thoughts can help to improve low mood and other symptoms of depression. However, this process alone may not be sufficient to help an individual to recover completely from depression and prevent it from happening again in the future. Even after individuals recover from depression, they are likely to remain vulnerable to relapse or recurrence of depression unless their psychological vulnerabilities to depression are dealt with effectively. In order to reduce the likelihood of a relapse or recurrence of depression, it is important to address psychological vulnerabilities by focusing on weakening individuals' key unhelpful assumptions on which their negative automatic thoughts are based.

Towards the end of cognitive therapy for depression, the therapeutic focus shifts from addressing current symptoms of depression to identifying and challenging unhelpful assumptions (see chapter 6 for further descriptions of unhelpful assumptions). A major advantage of cognitive therapy is that it can assist individuals in reducing the risk of relapse or recurrence of depression by changing unhelpful assumptions. In this chapter, we will describe the cognitive therapy strategies and techniques used to identify and change unhelpful assumptions. We will start by describing the origins of unhelpful assumptions, that is, from where these unhelpful assumptions are thought to originate and the various reasons for this. Then we will focus on specific strategies designed to help in the process of identifying and challenging unhelpful assumptions linked to depression. This chapter is based on the work of Aaron T. Beck and colleagues.[1]

## Origins of unhelpful assumptions

According to cognitive theory and therapy, the upsurge of negative automatic thoughts experienced when one is depressed tends to result from long-standing unhelpful assumptions. Therefore, once the symptoms of depression, particularly negative automatic thoughts, have lessened and the individual is better equipped to identify and challenge these thoughts, then therapeutic work on addressing unhelpful assumptions can begin. So, where do unhelpful assumptions come from? According to Beck and colleagues, unhelpful assumptions are learned during our developmental period. Unhelpful assumptions can result from childhood experiences, the beliefs, attitudes or rules of peers, parents or significant people in our lives, and family rules or traditions. Once developed, unhelpful assumptions tend to be culturally reinforced. For instance, Peter, a person who used to suffer from significant episodes of depression, remembers being told by his father 'If you don't do your best, you will get nowhere in life.' After repeating and mentally rehearsing this message to himself several times, Peter developed the unhelpful assumption 'Unless I am always best at what I do, I am not good enough.' Once an individual has developed unhelpful assumptions, these then tend to be used like 'formulas' or guides to behaviour and understanding the world. Unhelpful assumptions can guide the individual's thinking, memory, perception, attention, goals, ambitions, behaviour and emotions, and provide a general framework for understanding or interpreting events or situations that the individual experiences in life. Peter's unhelpful assumptions were contributing to him adopting thinking styles that were all-or-nothing or black-and-white in nature, rigid and inflexible, negative and catastrophic (for further details, see chapter 6). His memory was focused on what he considered to be important rules and high standards of performance, and also on the negative consequences of not maintaining these standards or failing to achieve. Peter's attention was very much focused on detail and the prevention of errors or mistakes. His goals and ambitions revolved around achievements, performance and avoiding failure. Peter's behaviour was designed to ensure that he would always get things right, maintain high standards and avoid all forms of criticism. Understandably, the way his unhelpful assumptions were used as guides to the world meant that Peter would experience a range of negative emotions including low mood, fear, anxiety, guilt, disappointment, anger, etc.

We are not fully aware of our unhelpful assumptions. For a great deal of the time, unhelpful assumptions are somewhat hidden and are unarticulated or non-verbalized to the individual. Although we may not be completely aware of these unhelpful assumptions, we might be aware of the things we do to satisfy their terms. For instance, Peter was clearly aware that whilst he was trying to get 'everything' right and maintain his high standards of behaviour and performance, his mood and emotions felt stable. Therefore, Peter was working hard to meet the terms of his assumptions. After all, it is very much like a 'personal contract' that we have with these unhelpful assumptions. However, Peter was also aware when he was not satisfying the terms of these assumptions. For instance, when he had difficulties dealing with the normal behaviour of his young children, meeting tight deadlines, receiving criticism in a constructive way, and being overwhelmed with tasks at work, Peter would experience significant anxiety and apprehension, which would often lead to self-criticism, rumination, and low mood. In this way, Peter felt that he was not meeting the terms of his personal contract with his unhelpful assumptions. In fact, Peter would see these difficulties as clear violations of his personal contract with his unhelpful assumptions.

Although for most of the time unhelpful assumptions appear hidden, a critical or significant event can trigger these assumptions, leading them to surface and contribute to episodes of depression. For instance, Peter's first episode of clinical depression developed soon after he was unable to secure a long-awaited and eagerly expected promotion at work. Peter interpreted this event as him failing to produce the best possible performance to achieve the promotion, hence seeing himself as not being good enough. As you read this, you might think that Peter was, as he put it himself, 'justified to become depressed' given the incident. However, it is important to be aware of the fact that Peter had been promoted to a very high senior level two months prior to applying for another promotion.

Several specific unhelpful assumptions may lead individuals to experience episodes of depression.[2] Some examples of these assumptions include: 'In order to be happy, I have to be successful in whatever I undertake'; 'To be happy, I must be accepted by all people at all times'; 'If I make a mistake, it means that I am inept'; 'I cannot live without you'; 'If somebody disagrees with me, it means that he or she does not like me', and 'My value as a person depends on what others think of me'. When individuals are depressed, unfortunately, they are not likely to question the reality or truth behind their unhelpful assumptions, and the longer they are depressed, the greater their belief or conviction about their assumptions. Individuals with depression are likely to see their unhelpful assumptions as facts rather than views or opinions that they have formed earlier on in life as a result of their experiences. According to Beck and colleagues,[1] unhelpful assumptions are 'as much a part of an individual's identity as being a male or a female.' Therefore, in cognitive therapy for depression, it is crucial to address individuals' unhelpful assumptions in order to help them to recover fully and prevent future depressions.

## Identifying unhelpful assumptions

Many common themes or messages can be found in the unhelpful assumptions of individuals with depression. However, although there are common themes running through these assumptions, each individual has a unique set of assumptions. Therefore, initial endeavours focus on identifying these specific sets of unhelpful assumptions. A useful starting point in identifying unhelpful assumptions is to recognize that they have certain unique characteristics including: (1) they fail to reflect the reality of all human experience; (2) they are rigid, overgeneralized and extreme; (3) instead of making it possible, they make it even harder to achieve our goals in life; (4) as we saw in the case of Peter, violating the terms of our personal contract with our unhelpful assumptions can lead to extreme and excessive emotions, such as depression and despair rather than sadness or regret, but when the terms are met, this is associated with extreme and excessive positive emotions, such as elation rather than pleasure; and (5) everyday experiences do not generally re-shape the nature of these unhelpful assumptions. Given the common themes running through unhelpful assumptions, it can also be useful to be aware of the groupings of these unhelpful assumptions or the main areas of concern in the process of identifying them. Beck and colleagues have grouped unhelpful assumptions in terms of three main areas of concern: achievement (high standards of performance, the need to succeed, etc.), acceptance (the need to be liked, loved, etc.), and control (the need to control events, the need to be strong, etc.).

Identifying unhelpful assumptions can be much more difficult than detecting negative automatic thoughts because unhelpful assumptions are not clearly articulated or verbalized and they are like generalized rules, which may never have been expressed in so many words. Therefore, the process of identifying unhelpful assumptions by individuals with depression will require considerable insight and exploration. Instead of jumping to conclusions about an individual's unhelpful assumptions, it is often helpful to start by inferring or developing hypotheses (or proposing explanations) about what these assumptions might be. Given that some earlier therapeutic work would have focused on identifying and challenging negative automatic thoughts, it might be helpful to infer or identify unhelpful assumptions from these thoughts. Several common themes might have emerged from negative automatic thoughts during earlier treatment sessions. For instance, a common theme emerging from Peter's negative automatic thoughts was concern about meeting work deadlines (e.g. 'I must complete tasks on time'; 'If I fail to submit my work on time, it would be bad news'; 'I cannot rest until a task is completed on time'). It is apparent that themes from Peter's negative automatic thoughts include performance and perfectionistic standards. In this way, Peter's verbalized unhelpful assumption is 'If I do not complete tasks on time, I am not good enough.'

The types of cognitive distortions or thinking errors contained within negative automatic thoughts can also be used as clues to unhelpful assumptions. Cognitive distortions and thinking errors in negative automatic thoughts may also reflect similar errors in unhelpful assumptions. For instance, Peter's negative automatic thoughts were particularly characterized by all-or-nothing or back-and-white thinking, which is a tendency to place all experiences or personal qualities into one of two extreme categories, such as success or failure, or good or bad, ignoring the 'grey' areas in between. When depressed, people tend to place themselves in the extreme negative category. In Peter's case, his unhelpful assumptions concerning performance and perfectionistic standards would bias his thinking and make him view himself as being either not good enough or completely useless/incompetent.

Often, the global and general evaluations that individuals with depression make about themselves can provide clues to their unhelpful assumptions. Peter used to evaluate himself as being 'stupid', a 'loser', and 'inept'. These global self-evaluations reflected Peter's unrelenting standards of behaviour, which were closely linked to his unhelpful assumptions.

Although cognitive therapy is primarily concerned with the 'here and now', important incidents from the past, family sayings and memories may lead to the discovery of unhelpful assumptions. Peter used to have some very vivid memories of certain childhood experiences. He used to remember panicking about going home after exam results were published in his school. He remembered feeling very anxious about his father asking him about the details of his results. Unless the outcome was '100 per cent', which is rarely the case for the vast majority of students taking any exams, Peter's father used to say to him 'Unless you achieve 100 per cent or do a lot better than this, you are no good, or you will have nowhere to go in life.' In addition, as we previously discussed, extreme and excessive positive or negative emotions are often a reflection of the unhelpful assumptions being satisfied or violated. Questioning about one's thinking during episodes of extreme and excessive positive or negative emotions may lead to discovering the individual's basic unhelpful assumptions.

A further strategy used in identifying unhelpful assumptions is to complete a questionnaire called the Dysfunctional Attitude Scale (DAS).[3] The DAS identifies unhelpful assumptions by asking the respondent to rate the extent to which they agree with a number of specific statements such as: 'People will probably think less of me if I make a mistake'; 'I must be a useful, productive, creative person or life has no purpose'; If you cannot do something well, there is little point in doing it at all, etc.

Finally, using the downward arrow technique can help to uncover underlying unhelpful assumptions.[4] This technique involves focusing on specific negative automatic thoughts, and rather than questioning or challenging these thoughts themselves, a number of questions can be repeated until it is possible to express a general statement that covers all situations where the same rules might be operating. Box 7.1 shows an example of the downward arrow technique used to assist Peter in identifying his unhelpful assumptions. Appendix 3 provides a template for using the downward arrow technique.

## Challenging unhelpful assumptions

As we have seen from previous sections of this chapter, identifying unhelpful assumptions is the first step in changing them. Therefore, once unhelpful assumptions have been clearly identified and verbalized, and they no longer appear to be 'hidden', their unhelpfulness and dysfunctionality becomes more apparent, and specific forms of questioning or challenging them, and behavioural experimentation, can then be used to find new, more moderate and realistic assumptions. In order to achieve this, cognitive therapy relies on a variety of arguments and exercises designed to help individuals with depression

Box 7.1. An example of the downward arrow technique

Negative automatic thought: I'm not going to be
able to do the task perfectly

↓

Supposing you don't, what would it mean to you?

↓

It will cause serious trouble and lead to bad things

↓

Supposing that happens, what then?

↓

People would be extremely angry and critical of me

↓

And supposing that was true, what would it mean to you?

↓

They will think I can't do my job

↓

Supposing they did that, what would it mean to you as a
person?

↓

I am not good enough
Unhelpful assumption: Unless I do things perfectly, I am
not good enough

closely determine the validity of their unhelpful assumptions. This task can be achieved effectively because individuals with depression can provide a rich source of information, which they can then use to challenge their unhelpful assumptions. However, it is important to note that change in unhelpful assumptions does not just occur because of the number of arguments generated against unhelpful assumptions. Instead, it is the specific pointed questioning and the particular arguments that make sense to individuals and assist in the process of changing unhelpful assumptions. Many of the strategies and techniques used to challenge negative automatic thoughts can also be used to change unhelpful assumptions. However, the best evidence or counter-arguments against unhelpful assumptions are those generated by individuals themselves or by them in close collaboration with the cognitive therapist. Specific questions, generation of counter-arguments, and suggestions of alternative assumptions are effective means of challenging unhelpful assumptions, rather than basic forms of lecture or simple verbal persuasion. To this end, Beck and colleagues[1, 5] suggest a number of questions that can be used to challenge unhelpful assumptions. A list of these questions can be found in box 7.2.

Box 7.2 Some questions for challenging unhelpful assumptions

1. In what way is the assumption unreasonable? Does the assumption fit the way the world works?
2. Does the assumption help you to get what you want out of life? Or does it hinder you?
3. What are the advantages and disadvantages of having your unhelpful assumptions?
4. Where does your unhelpful assumption come from? Does understanding how your unhelpful assumptions were formed help you to distance yourself from them?
5. What would be a more moderate alternative, which would confer the advantages of the unhelpful assumption without its disadvantages? Can you think of alternative ways of looking at your unhelpful assumption?
6. Is your unhelpful assumption extreme in its demands?
7. What is the long- versus short-term utility of your unhelpful assumptions?
8. What cognitive distortions or thinking errors (e.g. 'should' statements; all-or-nothing thinking; overgeneralization, etc.) do your unhelpful assumptions contain?

Some examples and applications of specific questions used to challenge unhelpful assumptions will now follow. A common and recurrent theme in the unhelpful assumptions of individuals with depression is the cognitive distortion or thinking error labelled 'should' statements. This implies that the assumption is true and it applies to all situations. For instance, Peter used to frequently mentally compare what he 'should' do with what he 'is' doing. In this way, Peter would usually judge his behaviour and himself to be inadequate in terms of his high and unrelenting standards. Beck and colleagues suggest a variation of a behavioural strategy used in the treatment of obsessive-compulsive disorder, referred to as response prevention, as a means of modifying the cognitive distortions or thinking errors in the form of 'shoulds'. They suggest guiding the individual to: (1) verbalizing the 'should' (e.g. 'I should never make any mistakes in my work'); (2) predicting what would happen if the 'should' was not followed (e.g., 'People will be very angry and critical of me'); (3) carrying out a behavioural experiment to test the prediction (e.g., deliberately making some mistakes in my work and later discovering that nobody was angry and critical); and (4) attempting to revise the rule on the basis of the results of this experiment (e.g. 'It's not necessary to produce perfect or mistake-free work'). Often, what individuals discover, as Peter did in the previous example, is that the outcome is not catastrophic and the arbitrariness of the unhelpful assumption becomes more apparent. In this way, individuals discover that the arbitrariness of their assumptions stops them from seeing and making the most of their own successes, setting priorities as to what they 'must' do next, and making decisions about what they want to do for themselves. Ultimately, this method allows for the unhelpful assumptions to be changed and revised.

Unhelpful assumptions give rise to a range of cognitive distortions. Becoming aware of the relevant cognitive distortions associated with particular unhelpful assumptions can help in questioning the validity of these assumptions. For example, Peter's negative automatic thoughts and unhelpful assumptions were characterized by all-or-nothing thinking, which involves thinking everything is either one extreme or another (black or white; good or bad, etc.). This form of all-or-nothing thinking in unhelpful assumptions can be modified in the same way as other assumptions. For instance, given the cognitive distortion of all-or-nothing thinking, it can be demonstrated that events may be evaluated on a continuum. That is, most things do not exist as extreme entities such as success or failure. In fact, there are shades of grey between these two concepts of success or failure into which we tend to fall. Peter learnt that the criteria of his cognitive distortions contained within his unhelpful assumptions were vague, open-ended, and highly arbitrary. Therefore, many other unhelpful assumptions can be modified in the same way.

Another useful strategy to challenge unhelpful assumptions is to list the advantages and disadvantages of having a particular assumption and then to attempt to correct any cognitive distortions in the list. Although this appears to be overly simple, according to Beck and colleagues it has been shown to be one of the most effective ways to modify unhelpful assumptions of individuals with depression in the long-term. Box 7.3 shows Peter's list of advantages and disadvantages of believing that 'Unless I am always best at what I do, I am not good enough.'

As we have seen so far, in the same way as with negative automatic thoughts, attempts to change or challenge unhelpful assumptions through sets of specific questions, counter-arguments, and generation of alternative assumptions or explanations can be very helpful. We have found that if individuals with depression continue to question the validity of their unhelpful assumptions, they become significantly less prone to

Box 7.3. Peter's list of advantages and disadvantages of his particular assumption

| Advantages of having this assumption | Disadvantages of having this assumption |
|---|---|
| (1) It has helped me do well in the past | (1) It puts me under constant stress and pressure |
| (2) It keeps me focused and motivated | (2) It severely affects my physical and mental health |
| (3) It has helped me avoid some troubles and problems | (3) It interferes with my personal and professional relationships |
| (4) It has stopped me from becoming a weak and complacent person | (4) It stops me from having any fun and leisure activities |
| | (5) It prevents me from being happy for good periods of time |
| | (6) It makes me give others a hard time |

experiencing future depressions. However, as with negative automatic thoughts, verbal challenging or questioning of unhelpful assumptions should always be tested and reinforced by changes in behaviour. Therefore, individuals with depression are encouraged to actively challenge their unhelpful assumptions on a day-to-day basis. Behavioural experiments may well need to be repeated over a more lengthy period of time than experiments relating to specific negative automatic thoughts, and also in a wider variety of situations. Once the unhelpful assumptions have been identified, individuals are encouraged to act against their unhelpful assumptions. This is perhaps one of the most effective ways to change unhelpful assumptions. For instance, Peter's fears and concerns about making mistakes were actively challenged by asking him to seek out situations in which there was a high probability of him making mistakes, and then carefully and objectively evaluate the outcome of this in relation to his long-held unhelpful assumptions. Cognitive therapists may also propose that individuals who feel compelled to be with others try and encourage themselves to be alone. Moreover, behavioural experiments to test unhelpful assumptions might involve individuals who place the highest value on acceptance to go to places where the probability of being accepted is slight. Individuals usually discover that they can act against their unhelpful assumptions at a gradual rate or straightaway. This will clearly lead to discomfort but, ultimately, acting against unhelpful assumptions becomes easier and leads to helpful discoveries about our world and ourselves.

## Key points covered in this chapter

- To reduce the likelihood of a relapse or recurrence of depression, it is important to address psychological vulnerabilities by focusing on weakening individuals' key unhelpful assumptions on which their negative automatic thoughts are based.
- Although for most of the time unhelpful assumptions appear hidden, a critical or significant event can trigger these assumptions, leading them to surface and contribute to episodes of depression.
- Unhelpful assumptions have certain unique and specific characteristics including: (1) they fail to reflect the reality of all human experience; (2) they are rigid, overgeneralized and extreme; (3) instead of making it possible, they make it even harder to achieve our goals in life; (4) violating the terms of our personal contract with our unhelpful assumptions can lead to extreme and excessive emotions, such as depression and despair rather than sadness or regret, but when the terms are met, this is associated with extreme and excessive positive emotions, such as elation rather than

pleasure; and (5) everyday experiences do not generally re-shape the nature of these unhelpful assumptions.

- Unhelpful assumptions can be identified by developing hypotheses about what they might be, inferring from previous negative automatic thoughts, examining cognitive distortions and thinking errors in negative automatic thoughts, looking at important incidents from the past, family sayings and memories, completing the Dysfunctional Attitudes Scale, and using the downward arrow technique.

- Specific questions, generation of counter-arguments, suggestions of alternative assumptions, and behavioural experimentation are effective means of challenging unhelpful assumptions.

# 8

# Changing how you feel by changing how you relate

When people become depressed, they can experience difficulties in social and interpersonal circumstances or relationship problems with other people in their lives. Similarly, difficulties in social and interpersonal circumstances can also lead to people experiencing symptoms of depression. People with depression can be helped to address these circumstances and improve their symptoms through a psychological treatment called Interpersonal Psychotherapy (IPT). Like cognitive and behavioural therapies, IPT is a specific, time-limited and effective therapy that is designed to address the needs of individuals with depression. It was originally developed by Gerald L. Klerman, Myrna M. Weissman and a number of collaborators.[1, 2] Although IPT was initially created for the treatment of clinical depression, it has more recently been adapted to address the needs of individuals with a number of other problems, including anxiety and eating disorders.[3]

In this chapter, we provide a description of the origins and definition of IPT, its goals and characteristics, and how these goals can be achieved in helping people overcome their depression through the different therapeutic phases of IPT. In doing so, we hope that the reader will not only learn more about another effective psychological treatment for depression, but also acquire some specific strategies and techniques to begin to address their symptoms of depression or those of someone else who might be suffering from depression. This chapter is based entirely on the IPT for depression work by Klerman, Weissman, Markowitz and colleagues, which is fully referenced in the chapter notes.

## Origins and definition of IPT

The psychological theory and treatment of IPT have three important bases.[1,2,3] First, IPT pays close attention to the quality of our relationships or attachments to significant people, because these are seen as necessary for our well-being. When our attachment needs are not met (e.g. not receiving sufficient emotional warmth and affection because we find ourselves in regular conflict with our loved ones), we tend to experience psychological difficulties and a breakdown of our social and interpersonal relationships. This is why, as research has shown, adequate social support and intimacy can protect us against depression and other difficulties in the face of stress. Second, early negative life experiences, such as traumas, abuse, neglect, etc., can influence whether or not individuals can meet their own needs and thrive psychologically. These experiences can contribute to people becoming vulnerable to a number of emotional and psychological difficulties in adult life. Such difficulties could, for instance, take the form of social or interpersonal problems, which can lead to people developing depression. Finally, IPT is also based on research showing that when people become depressed there are usually problematic social or interpersonal circumstances, which might either have contributed to their depression or resulted from it. Understanding the research and theoretical basis of IPT may help in understanding its goals, strategies and techniques more clearly.

According to IPT, depression usually occurs in a social and interpersonal context. That is to say, regardless of what may have caused the depression, it is usually related to problematic social and interpersonal circumstances. For example, people become depressed in the context of a loved one dying, a dispute between you and a significant person in your life, a dissolution of a friendship, the break-up of a marriage, children leaving home (the 'empty nest syndrome'), a new job, the loss of a job, a job promotion, a move to a new neighbourhood, etc. Therefore, the social and interpersonal context of depression is at the therapeutic heart of IPT. That is, by understanding what was happening in your personal life, socially or interpersonally, and usually with significant people around the time when you became depressed, you will learn to address the symptoms of your depression. According to IPT, to be able to address these symptoms, we need to understand that depression has three parts: your symptoms of depression, your social and interpersonal life (i.e. how you relate to important people in your life such as partner, spouse, children, family, friends, colleagues, etc.), and your personality (i.e. how your personality traits influence how you relate to others, how these traits may have contributed to the development of your depression and how you cope with its symptoms). Note that although IPT pays close attention to an individual's personality, it does not attempt to change it, but instead it aims to improve the individual's depression and the way he or she functions socially or interpersonally.

## Goals and characteristics of IPT

IPT shares the same basic therapeutic goal as other effective psychological therapies for depression. This goal is to understand, alleviate and prevent symptoms of depression. However, instead of achieving this goal through behavioural or cognitive means, IPT examines how the symptoms of depression relate to the individual's current social and personal life, uses specific strategies and techniques to solve these problems and, in turn, addresses the symptoms of depression. In doing so, IPT aims to help people with depression cope better with difficult social and interpersonal circumstances and improve their quality of life.

IPT has a number of important characteristics. These include the following: IPT is time-limited and short rather than long term; it is focused (i.e. it aims to address one or two current social and interpersonal problem areas) rather than being open-ended; and it focuses on the 'here and now' rather than the 'there and then' (i.e. the past) of a person's social and interpersonal relationships.

In delivering IPT to individuals with depression, a number of strategies and techniques are used. The IPT strategies, which are the main elements of this treatment, are described in detail in the next sections of this chapter. A number of IPT techniques are used to help individuals with depression. The individual's interpersonal problem area will determine the order and frequency of use of these techniques. Some techniques are exploratory because they involve carefully collecting information about symptoms of depression by using general and open-ended questions or more direct or specific enquiries into a new topic. Another important group of therapeutic techniques aims to encourage people with depression to express their emotions better and learn to adopt an attitude of acceptance of painful feelings. Clarification is used to repeat, rephrase or emphasize important material discussed in the session. A key and commonly used IPT technique that is designed to help individuals communicate more effectively by, for instance, exploring and recognizing communication failures, is referred to as communication analysis. For example, if an individual expresses their thoughts or emotions in an ambiguous, indirect and non-verbal way as a substitute for open confrontation, this can lead to the initiation or maintenance of a dispute or disagreement with others, which can either generate symptoms of depression or make existing symptoms worse. The use of the patient–therapist relationship is another important technique in IPT. To bring about change in a depressed individual's behaviour, a number of specific techniques may be used, including educating, advising, 'modelling' or practical demonstrations of desired behaviours, or assisting individuals in solving relatively simple, straightforward practical problems. An especially important technique that is designed to assist the individual in considering a range of alternative actions and their consequences in order to solve a specific problem is referred to as decision analysis. Understanding how individuals feel and communicate with others, and practising new behaviours in social and interpersonal interactions involves role-playing. Finally, some additional IPT techniques include contract setting, which involves an agreement of specific tasks to be undertaken throughout treatment and also in defining and clarifying the role of the patient and the therapist in this process, as well as administrative details such as appointment times.

The appropriately trained and experienced IPT therapist plays a number of key roles in this treatment. Although some of these roles are not specific to IPT, as they also apply to other psychological treatments such as behavioural and cognitive interventions, IPT places particular emphasis on the role of the therapist and the relationship between the patient and the therapist. In addition to gathering important information and understanding the individual's depression, IPT therapists may offer advice or make suggestions for coping better with the social and interpersonal difficulties related to depression. Moreover, IPT therapists are seen as the patient's advocate and they are not neutral. Therefore, they will have the depressed individual's interests at heart and will make every effort to understand their current life situation from their point of view. The patient–therapist relationship is crucial in IPT. This relationship is of a therapeutic nature rather than a friendship. Finally, an important role of the IPT therapist is to remain active rather than passive throughout treatment, hence attempting to help individuals improve their current social and interpersonal situation and alleviate their symptoms of depression.

## Therapeutic phases of IPT

IPT progresses through three separate therapeutic phases. The first phase involves the initial treatment sessions, which are designed to assess the nature of the individual's presenting problems, establish a diagnosis and guide the focus of future treatment sessions. During the second phase, the aim is to work on the chosen problematic interpersonal areas, including grief (complicated bereavement), interpersonal role disputes, role transitions and interpersonal sensitivity. The therapeutic work that takes place in each one of these areas will be discussed in detail later. In the final phase, the patient and therapist work together to summarize the work carried out, consolidate therapeutic gains and plan to prevent relapse or recurrence of depressive symptoms.

During the initial IPT sessions, attempts are made to establish whether individuals present with symptoms of depression so that a clinical diagnosis of major depressive disorder can be made. A physical examination may be required or recommended in order to rule out any possible physical explanations for the person's symptoms of depression. If the results of any physical investigations prove the absence of specific medical causes for the symptoms, then the IPT therapist will attempt to explain the diagnosis and treatment of depression. In the initial phase, the IPT therapist will also attempt to establish if there is a need for medication since this is another effective option in the treatment of depression. A number of specific medical considerations will help to establish whether medication is prescribed or not, such as how severe the person's symptoms of depression might be. Following these initial tasks, attempts are made to determine what was going on in the person's social and interpersonal life when they became depressed. This task is crucial in guiding future IPT sessions. Relating depression to the depressed person's current social and interpersonal problems may involve finding out who the key persons in his or her life are and what exactly was happening at the time when they started to feel depressed at work, at home, with their family, friends, etc. The IPT therapist may ask individuals with depression to complete the interpersonal questionnaire to help determine the specific social and interpersonal problem areas, because it is one or two of these areas which will be chosen to work on during the second phase of IPT. The interpersonal questionnaire encourages the individual to think about what was going on in his or her life at the time when they became depressed and answer a number of questions including: Did something upsetting happen? Did someone close to you die? were you having problems at home with your partner? Were you having problems at work? Had anything changed in your life? Towards the end of these initial IPT sessions, a treatment contract is established and the patient is informed about what to expect in treatment. On completion of this initial phase, the second phase begins and specific IPT strategies are used to address one or possibly two interpersonal problem areas. Each of these interpersonal problem areas is described in detail below.

## Grief (complicated bereavement)

If the symptoms of depression developed in relation to the death of a loved one and the individual is experiencing difficulties coming to terms with it, grief or complicated bereavement is chosen as an interpersonal problem area to focus on in IPT. Grief reactions can be normal or complicated and the focus of IPT is on treating episodes of depression related to complicated grief reactions. Complicated grief reactions tend to result from an individual's difficulties in going through the various phases of the normal mourning process. Box 8.1 describes the differences between normal and complicated grief.

Box 8.1  Normal versus complicated grief

### Normal grief

Individuals who experience normal grief reactions share some of the signs, symptoms or difficulties that are experienced by those with clinical depression including sadness or low mood, lack of interest or pleasure, appetite/weight loss and difficulty sleeping. However, normal grief reactions are not the same as episodes of depression. The key symptoms and difficulties experienced during normal grief reactions tend to improve without professional help or treatment in about two to four months as the individual progresses through the various phases of the normal mourning process and the individual becomes more fully aware of the reality of the loss or death. Normal grief reactions do not generally require medical or psychological interventions since they are not viewed as medical conditions.

### Complicated grief

Complicated grief reactions tend to occur when the initial signs, symptoms or difficulties associated with the death of a loved one are severe, last more than two months, interfere

*Continued*

> with a person's functioning, and grief does not occur or is postponed and then experienced in a much more severe form long after the loved one has died. Complicated grief reactions can lead to episodes of depression, and when they do, they require professional help and treatment.

In essence, the goals of IPT for addressing episodes of depression associated with complicated grief reactions are to assist the individual in overcoming difficulties and progressing through the various phases of the normal mourning process, and in re-establishing new interests and forming satisfying new relationships with others that may help to replace or substitute for what was lost. In order to achieve this, a number of IPT strategies are used. For instance, individuals with depression may be encouraged to think and talk openly about the loss of the loved one and express emotions or feelings about this experience as they discuss the sequence and consequence of events before, during and after the death. Sally entered IPT soon after her husband had died from cancer. Treatment progressed with detailed discussions of all of the events surrounding the death of her husband. Although she found it very difficult and upsetting to talk about these events, it gave her the opportunity to start going through the mourning process with the support of the IPT therapist.

Individuals will also be encouraged to discuss the nature of the relationship to the dead person and any changes or consequences experienced since the death or loss. Sally was asked questions such as 'What was your husband like?' and 'What things have changed since he passed away?' This may also involve looking at old picture albums with friends or family, or perhaps seeing old friends or acquaintances who knew the dead person. Sally was able to look at old and more recent holiday pictures with both the therapist and friends, and was helped to explore previous experiences with her husband. During discussions, the IPT therapist may also encourage the individual to talk about the experiences he or she did or did not like within the relationship. For instance, Sally was encouraged to consider questions such as 'What did you do together?', 'What did you like the most/least?' and 'What were the good/bad things?' This helped Sally to view her past relationship with her husband in a more realistic and less idealized way.

The IPT therapist may offer reassurance to the individual that any fears they express are common and part of the normal mourning process. This certainly was important in the case of Sally as her symptoms were contributing to her feeling detached or removed from her world and thinking 'I'm losing control'. It was crucial to help Sally understand these experiences as normal and view them as part of her symptoms and normal process of mourning. Overall, the IPT therapist helps the individual to develop a clear picture of the relationship with the person they lost, which is more balanced and perhaps less idealized, and one that includes both good and bad points.

## Interpersonal role disputes

If the symptoms of depression were started by or are maintained by an interpersonal dispute, then this problem area becomes the focus of IPT. An interpersonal dispute can occur when an individual and at least one other significant person in his or her life has different expectations about the relationship, which gives rise to tension, conflict and disagreement. For example, Stephanie's problems of depression revolved around a role dispute with her husband. She felt that her husband did not appreciate at all her input into the care of their two children and her regular home management activities, despite her extensive efforts and dedication.

The goals of IPT for treating depression that centres on interpersonal disputes consist of: (1) identifying the dispute;

(2) generating solutions and a plan of action; and (3) changing any unhelpful communication patterns or expectations, or both, in order to reach a resolution of the dispute. IPT for depression in the context of interpersonal disputes is often similar to couples/marital therapy.

In identifying the interpersonal dispute, the IPT therapist will consider three possible stages: impasse (dead end), re-negotiation or dissolution. Impasse means that discussions between the individual and an important person in their life have ended and there might be low-level resentment, which may be characteristic of 'cold marriages', but there are no endeavours to try to re-negotiate the relationship. During the re-negotiation stage, although the individual and the significant other might be able to acknowledge openly their differences, they are also actively engaging in endeavours to change the situation, even if initially unsuccessfully. The third stage of an interpersonal dispute, referred to as dissolution, means that the relationship is irretrievably disrupted by the dispute and the efforts focus on terminating the relationship through divorce, separation or perhaps by abandoning a difficult work situation. Although the quality of Stephanie's relationship with her husband was rather poor, they were both mindful of their differences and tried several times, albeit unsuccessfully, to bring about change. This lack of progress appeared to be due to ineffective means of communicating about their feelings and a range of problems.

Communication analysis, a specific IPT technique discussed earlier, is often used to address impasse or re-negotiation in order to help individuals learn new, more helpful, appropriate or effective ways of communicating to bring about dispute resolution. Communication analysis essentially assists the individual in developing new and better ways of dealing with the disagreement. Stephanie learned specific ways of verbally communicating more effectively with her husband, such as avoiding sulking when angry, expressing her needs and feelings clearly and openly rather than expecting her husband to anticipate these all the time, and seeking feedback as well as clarification about any issues discussed. This strategy led to improved communication between them as well as improvements in her symptoms of depression.

IPT for depression in the context of an interpersonal dispute at the stage of dissolution is very similar to IPT for depression that centres on a complicated grief reaction in that it helps the individual to progress through the various phases of the normal loss process and view the relationship in a more balanced and perhaps less idealized way, so that they are able to distance themselves from that person and develop new satisfying relationships. Another specific IPT technique, decision analysis, is also used for addressing interpersonal disputes as it assists the individual in considering a wider range of alternative actions, and the consequences of many different actions, before they make a decision.

## Role transitions

If the symptoms of depression were started or are maintained by a role transition or life change that the individual has difficulties coping with, then role transitions are considered an interpersonal problem area to focus on in IPT. Important life changes include divorce, loss of leisure following the birth of a child, moving house, changing jobs, leaving home, economic change, changes in family roles due to illness, new responsibilities, etc. For example, Mark's depression developed a few weeks after his retirement.

According to IPT, these changes can lead to depression if the individual has not realized what is expected in their new role. This is why an initial aim of IPT in addressing role transitions is to explore what the life change might mean to the individual in

terms of the demands of the new situation, and what the benefits and costs might be, since most transitions generally com-
prise both advantages and disadvantages. Mark was
encouraged to think about a number of important questions
including 'How did your life change after retiring?', 'How did
you feel about the change?', 'What was your life like before you
retired?', 'What people were left behind and what people took
their place?' Questions such as these helped Mark to acknowledge many advantages of his work, such as relationships with
colleagues and sense of achievement and job satisfaction.
However, Mark also recognized that there were a number of
disadvantages of his work (e.g. company conflicts and pressures, tensions between certain colleagues, etc.) and good
things about his new situation (e.g. more time to spend with his
family and friends, and to devote to hobbies and holidays, more
opportunities for community work, etc.).

If the transition is unexpected, undesired and the individual
is not prepared, the role transition would be more difficult and
the individual may feel more helpless or unable to cope with the
change. More specific difficulties in coping with role transitions may be related to the loss of social and emotional support,
dealing with negative emotions such as anger or fear, need for a
new range of social skills and low self-esteem. During the
course of IPT, Mark learned to develop new attachments and
relationships with others, and express and manage his anger
more effectively. Therefore, the goal of IPT for treating depression in the context of role transitions consists of the person giving up the old role, expressing negative emotions such as guilt,
anger and fears regarding the loss, acquiring and implementing
new skills such as social skills, developing new and satisfying
relationships and support groups, and becoming more aware
and acknowledging the benefits of the new role. This can effectively assist the individual in managing the role transition and
overcoming his or her symptoms of depression.

## Interpersonal sensitivity

If the symptoms of depression are related to a long-standing difficulty in finding or sustaining fulfilling interpersonal relationships and to overwhelming feelings of loneliness and social isolation, but not specifically related to some recent transition, then interpersonal sensitivity may be chosen as an interpersonal problem area to focus on in IPT. According to IPT, there are three groups of individuals who may have problems of interpersonal sensitivity: (1) individuals who are socially isolated and lack relationships with close or intimate friends or colleagues at work or who have a history of problems forming intimate or close relationships; (2) individuals who have an adequate number and range of relationships, but do not find them satisfying and have difficulties in maintaining these relationships (this may include individuals who have long-standing low self-esteem problems); and (3) individuals who have been depressed for a considerable period of time and still experience residual or lingering symptoms of depression, which might not have been treated or have been treated ineffectively in the past and continue to interfere with relationships. Jonathan was a successful businessman who lived on his own and spent a great deal of time feeling lonely and socially isolated. Although he knew a lot of people, his interpersonal relationships were generally superficial and he found it difficult to trust others.

The goal of IPT for depression in the context of interpersonal sensitivity is to reduce the individual's social isolation by improving social and interpersonal skills, boosting self-confidence, strengthening existing relationships, and forming new fulfilling and satisfying ones. The IPT therapist may focus on the individual's past relationships or the patient–therapist relationship, if the individual lacks significant and meaningful relationships in their life. There are three major tasks involved in addressing interpersonal problem areas characterized by interpersonal sensitivity: (1) carefully examining past significant relationships in terms of both positive and negative aspects; (2) identifying any recurrent or parallel problems in these relationships; and (3) encouraging the individual to discuss his or her negative and positive feelings about the IPT therapist and parallels in other relationships. IPT with Jonathan began with a detailed discussion of past and current relationships and he discovered a clear and consistent pattern in these relationships. Jonathan learned that he tended to be very controlling of others by, for instance, always wanting to make the decisions and determine what was right or wrong in a situation. He also realized that his father used to adopt similar attitudes with most people he knew. IPT focused on assisting Jonathan in changing his unhelpful tendencies and improving his social and interpersonal skills in current relationships through the use of role-playing and analyses of his styles of communication. He was also helped to learn effective means of meeting people and developing satisfying relationships without relying on previous negative patterns of interacting. Subsequently, Jonathan met a woman whom he was able to develop a close, trusting and intimate relationship.

## Final phase of IPT

As in other time-limited therapies, including behavioural and cognitive therapies, in IPT termination of treatment is specifically discussed a few sessions before it occurs. In order to facilitate the task of termination, the last three to four sessions involve: (1) specific review and discussion of the end of IPT treatment; (2) recognition and acknowledgement of the fact that the end of treatment can be a time of potential grieving; and (3) recognition of the individual's independent competence in dealing with problems. A review of what has and has not been accomplished during IPT sessions is also carried out at the end of treatment. If an individual is not ready, or does not want to terminate treatment, then there may be a mutual agreement to wait for several weeks to establish if further treatment is warranted. Clearly, if individuals continue to experience symptoms of depression or have not improved much through IPT, alternative treatments are discussed, including adding or changing medication, considering a different type of therapy, therapy with a different therapist or a re-negotiation of the therapeutic contract with the current IPT therapist. In order to prevent relapse or recurrence of depression, some individuals may also need to receive longer-term treatment and/or maintenance IPT. This may include individuals with long-standing histories of recurrent depression, ongoing problems in relationships, and those who have not shown much improvement and are still depressed. Ultimately, the emphasis of IPT is to help the individual to deal more successfully with their interpersonal life in terms of work, friendships, etc., outside of the treatment sessions.

During the final phase of IPT, the individual's sense of independent competence to address future problems is fostered by identifying areas of future work and exploring how effective solutions can be implemented. Importantly, individuals' future ability to determine whether or not further help is required is discussed in the last treatment session. Finally, if an individual's depression does not benefit from IPT, it is important to remember that it is the treatment that has failed rather than the individual. Fortunately, as can be seen in this book, a number of other helpful and effective treatments for depression do exist.

## Key points covered in this chapter

- Depression can lead to difficulties in social and interpersonal circumstances, but these circumstances can also contribute to people experiencing symptoms of clinical depression.

- In IPT, by understanding what was going on in your social or interpersonal life with significant people around the time when you became depressed, you will learn to address the symptoms of your depression.
- The goals of IPT are to examine how the symptoms of depression relate to the individual's current social and personal life, use strategies and techniques to solve these problems and, in turn, address the symptoms of depression and improve the individual's quality of life.
- During the second, and most important, therapeutic phase of IPT, the aim is to work on the chosen problematic interpersonal areas such as grief (complicated bereavement), interpersonal role disputes, role transitions and interpersonal sensitivity.
- If the symptoms of depression developed in relation to the death of a loved one and the individual is experiencing difficulties coming to terms with it, then grief or complicated bereavement is chosen as an interpersonal problem area to focus on in IPT.
- If the symptoms of depression were started or are maintained by an interpersonal role dispute, then this interpersonal problem area becomes the focus of IPT.
- If the symptoms of depression were started or are maintained by a role transition or life change that the individual has difficulties coping with, then role transitions are considered an interpersonal problem area to focus on in IPT.
- If the symptoms of depression are related to a long-standing difficulty in finding or sustaining fulfilling interpersonal relationships, and to overwhelming feelings of loneliness and social isolation, then interpersonal sensitivity may be chosen as an interpersonal problem area to focus on in IPT.
- Ultimately, the emphasis of IPT is to help the individual to deal more successfully with their interpersonal life in terms of work, friendships, etc., outside of the treatment sessions.

# 9

# Feeling well, staying well: preventing relapse and recurrence of depression

As we discussed in chapters 4 to 8, episodes of clinical depression can be overcome by effective psychological and pharmacological treatment. However, for a significant number of people, depression is a recurrent problem that threatens to return even after recovering from it. Indeed, research studies have found that many people who recover from an episode of depression tend to experience another one. It appears that the more episodes one has, the more likely it is that one will have future episodes. For example, people with a history of two or more previous episodes of depression have a 70–80 per cent likelihood of having another episode in their lifetime.[1] We want to reassure you that providing this information is not a form of scare tactics to increase anyone's fear of relapse and recurrence of depression. These are important facts that we want to share with you in a responsible way in order to help you to protect yourself from relapse or recurrence of depression. Once individuals are able to start to feel well and recover from depression, a crucial goal is to ensure that they stay well. The main aim of this chapter is to help you to improve your chances of remaining free of depression in the future.

This chapter reviews specific strategies aimed at maximizing the prevention of relapse and recurrence of depression. We start by discussing the factors found to determine whether or not individuals are likely to re-experience depression in the future. We then list a number of strategies and techniques that can be used after individuals have recovered from depression to stay well and to protect themselves from the return of depression. The excellent book written by clinical psychologists Peter Bieling and Martin Antony[2] has influenced several sections of this chapter.

## What makes depression return and how can it be prevented?

A number of factors can determine whether or not individuals are likely to experience a relapse or recurrence of depression. Some of these factors include the following: a history of past depressions (particularly at younger ages); certain personality styles and characteristics; having other psychological problems; frequent exposure to stress; low levels of social support; the presence of residual, mild symptoms of depression; and poor medication compliance. Therefore, a key to preventing the return of depression is to try to understand and address the factors that predict it.

Several strategies and techniques have been found to effectively reduce the likelihood of relapse and recurrence of depression. These strategies include: continuing to take maintenance medication; continuing to have 'booster' sessions of maintenance psychotherapy; remaining behaviourally active and healthy; continuing to challenge negative thinking; and continuing to relate well and develop healthy relationships. Other strategies that can be used to prevent the return of depression include the following: continuing to challenge unhelpful assumptions as well as personality styles; practising mindfulness meditation; and solving problems effectively. In the next sections of this chapter, we review the key strategies and techniques used to prevent relapse and recurrence of depression.

Before implementing methods designed to prevent the return of depression, it is important to ensure that the individual is free from depression for a specified period of time. To assess this, it is important to be familiar with two key concepts: remission and recovery. Full or partial remission refers to being completely free or partially free from symptoms of depression for at least two weeks or fourteen consecutive days. Recovery is a much longer period of remission, which lasts at least six months.[2] A psychiatrist or clinical psychologist can help to establish an individual's depression status. In addition, specific questionnaires, such as that presented in chapter 2 of this book, can help determine whether a person is still experiencing symptoms of depression, which may require further treatment before engaging in depression prevention. It is important to determine whether the individual should focus on treatment for a current episode of clinical depression or whether they are ready to start working towards staying well and preventing the return of depression.

## Staying well by continuing to take maintenance medication

Anti-depressant medication can help to treat episodes of depression and also prevent them from returning. As noted in chapter 4, poor medication adherence is a key factor in relapse/recurrence of depression. The key advantages of medication over psychological treatments for depression include the fact that they are easier to obtain and take, and their speed of action may be quicker than other forms of treatment. However, compared to other effective forms of treatment, the key disadvantages of medication include the fact that they may be more expensive in the long term and are sometimes associated with side effects and interactions with other medications. In addition, as mentioned in chapter 4, although some medications may be unsafe for people who have particular medical conditions or who want to get pregnant, psychiatrists who specialize in this field are able to offer specific advice on the best (in terms of safety and effectiveness) medication strategies to use to address these issues.

An important point to be aware of is the fact that the more severe one's depression, the more likely it is that one will need medication or a combination of medication and effective psychological treatment such as cognitive behavioural therapy (CBT) or interpersonal psychotherapy (IPT). Chapter 4 reviews the different stages of medication treatment, lists a number of medications that have been found to work for depression and suggests alternative medical treatments when particular medications might not work. A commonly asked question is how long one should continue to take medication or when one would be in a position to come off the medication. As discussed in chapter 4, for a number of individuals with depression, continuing to take medication for a long time may be the best option. For others, it may be difficult to reach a point at which they can come off their medication without experiencing relapse or recurrence of depression. Research has shown that continuing to take medication is particularly important for those who have experienced three or more episodes of clinical depression, have had one or two severe episodes, have chronic or long-lasting depressions, have a history of relapsing upon discontinuing their medication, have late onset depression (first episode after age fifty), and would find the relapse or recurrence of depression difficult to cope with.[3] What is really important is that the decision to come off anti-depressant medication should be made in consultation with your doctor or psychiatrist.

## Staying well by continuing 'booster' sessions of maintenance psychotherapy

As we have seen in chapters 5 to 8, effective psychological treatments such as CBT or IPT can help individuals recover from depression. However, ongoing psychological treatment or maintenance psychotherapy when one is well can be helpful for preventing relapse and staying depression-free over the longer term. Studies have shown that one of the most effective ways of staying depression-free is to combine medication and monthly CBT or IPT. A frequently asked question is whether one needs to have maintenance psychotherapy. Clearly, the answer to this question would vary from individual to individual and decisions should be carefully made in close consultation with the relevant healthcare professional.

There are several issues to consider in the process of determining whether or not one needs to have maintenance psychotherapy. Key issues include the risk level based on past depression, previous experiences with psychological treatments, one's compatibility with psychological treatments and the triggers for depression. If you choose to have maintenance psychotherapy, an important factor to be aware of is that your therapist, whether previous or new, has appropriate training, qualifications and experience in providing evidence-based psychological treatment in the form of CBT or IPT.

Another important frequently asked question if one decides to have maintenance psychotherapy is how often one should have the psychological treatment sessions. Clearly, the structure of your maintenance psychotherapy sessions should be decided in close collaboration with your therapist. Research studies have shown that monthly sessions may be sufficient for preventing the return of depression. The content of the maintenance psychotherapy sessions is another factor that should be agreed upon in close collaboration with your therapist. Personally relevant issues should be addressed at each meeting and you might find it helpful to work with your therapist on a wellness plan using the workbook written by Bieling and Antony.[2] In fact, these authors helpfully compare maintenance psychotherapy with the model of care a dentist might use:

> We visit the dentist regularly for checkups, even when our teeth look and feel just fine. This checkup involves some maintenance, cleaning, exaggerating to the hygienist about how often we floss, and a quick examination by the dentist to make sure nothing is cropping up that needs attention. Psychotherapy for people who are vulnerable to depression could follow this dentistry model even after monthly maintenance sessions are ended. A periodic checkup to delve into recent events, revisit your wellness plan and anticipate future hurdles may be a good idea. Also, just as you would go see the dentist if you suddenly had a toothache between checkups, you could schedule a session with your therapist if a stressor crops up or if you note a lasting downturn in your mood.
>
> P. J. Bieling and M. M. Antony (2003) *Ending the Depression Cycle: A Step-by-step Guide for Preventing Relapse.* California: New Harbinger Publications, p. 73–74.

## Staying well by remaining behaviourally active and healthy

As we saw in chapter 5, changing behaviour has been found to be very helpful in lifting the mood of individuals with depression. An effective approach to overcoming symptoms of depression and begin to feel well is behavioural activation. The key goal of behavioural activation is to examine everyday activities and life choices and start to become more behaviourally active and to look at the effect of new behaviours on mood and sense of pleasure and achievement. Carefully examining current behaviour and making small changes can have positive effects on mood. Behavioural activation not only helps individuals to recover from their depression, it can also assist them in staying well and preventing the return of depression. Maintaining sufficient levels of reward and reinforcement through daily activities when we feel well can help us to stay well and protect us from relapse or recurrence of depression.

Here is a brief summary for achieving optimal behavioural activation. The first step is to spend time closely examining current behaviour and how it affects mood. Activity monitoring can help us to become aware of habitual behaviour patterns, which might be keeping us inactive and at risk of low mood. Some useful tips for completing activity monitoring charts are described in chapter 5. After about a week of activity monitoring, try to examine all of your charts, looking for any patterns, such as particular times of the day, situations or activities that will link with you feeling more sad, or particular situations or activities that you found enjoyable or gave you a sense of achievement. Following this, the next step is to start making changes in your behaviour and planning new activities. There are several things to keep in mind when considering activity scheduling. One thing to bear in mind is to schedule activities that will have a positive, albeit small, impact on your mood. Another important issue to bear in mind when scheduling activities is to maintain a balance between enjoyable activities and those that give you a sense of achievement. This would help to reduce any overwhelming feelings. Balancing activities involves comparing your levels of pleasure and sense of achievement with one another. If you notice an imbalance in the direction of too much pleasure or too much achievement, then this needs to be adjusted. We do not assume that most people have a perfect balance between activities that give them a sense of pleasure and achievement. Given our current and daily demands and pressures, it is difficult to attain a perfectly balanced activity schedule. However, whenever possible, it is helpful to strive to achieve a good balance between these two rewards in our lives. Finally, in the process of planning ahead and carrying out helpful activity scheduling, it is important to consider reversing any avoidance (e.g. procrastination) and removing any activities from your life that do not contribute to a sense of pleasure or achievement. Specific steps to bear in mind in the process of overcoming avoidance are detailed in chapter 5.

In the process of examining everyday activities, it is important to consider two key daily activities, which have been linked to the occurrence of depression and to treatments for depression that have been shown to work. These activities are sleep and exercise. Sleep and exercise should be clearly incorporated in any activity scheduling plan. If you are vulnerable to relapses or recurrences of depression, it is vital that you ensure that your sleep rhythm is as regular and as restful as possible. Your daily activity scheduling should have sufficient room to schedule enough sleep time. The general consensus is that approximately eight hours of sleep should be sufficient, although some people require less and others require more. Whether you need more or less sleep time, you need to clearly schedule this in your plan. There are a number of basic rules for maintaining good sleep hygiene. These are summarized in box 9.1.

In addition to maintaining good sleep hygiene, it is important to exercise regularly. Exercise can offer our two key life rewards of pleasure and achievement. In addition, exercise can impact positively on both our physical and mental well-being.

Box 9.1 Basic rules for maintaining good sleep hygiene

1. Try to go to bed at the same time every day and try to get up at the same time every day.
2. Carefully monitor your consumption of alcohol and caffeine. Avoid using these substances to influence your sleep (i.e. caffeine to wake up and alcohol to go to sleep). Alcohol and caffeine should be restricted to no more than one dose per day, that is, one cup of coffee or one alcoholic drink per day.
3. Any form of emotional or significant physical stimulation before bedtime should be avoided. It is helpful to avoid or postpone any kind of strong emotion or challenging task or work before trying to sleep.
4. Try to create a comfortable sleeping environment for yourself. This includes the bed itself, having a quiet environment and darkness.
5. Try to avoid napping during the daytime even when you have not had a good night's sleep. It is important to remember that disturbing the sleep routine and napping to catch up can quickly become a vicious cycle.

Regular exercise can contribute to significant improvements in symptoms of depression. Exercise can also serve to prevent relapse and recurrence of depression. Therefore, exercise should be an important consideration in planning your daily activities and ensuring that you stay well. The key goal here is to obtain the desired effects from exercise on your mood and prevent depression. Three times a week of moderate exercise (brisk walking or slow jogging) that lasts between twenty and sixty minutes might be sufficient to benefit mood according to research. However, exercise should be maintained over the long term to ensure long-lasting mood benefits. Before you plan to incorporate regular exercise into your activity scheduling, it is advisable to consult with your doctor or a specialist sports/exercise professional as to whether this is something you can take up and incorporate into your routine.

## Staying well by continuing to challenge negative thinking

According to cognitive therapy, we feel the way we think. Therefore, changing the way we think can help us overcome an episode of depression. Research studies have found that monthly sessions of cognitive therapy for individuals who have recovered from depression could also substantially increase the probability of preventing the return of depression and staying well. In comparison to normal clinical management, cognitive therapy has been found to reduce the risk of relapse by half.

So how can cognitive therapy help individuals to stay well and prevent relapse or recurrence of depression? As we saw in chapter 6, the first step is to learn to recognize negative automatic thoughts when they go through your mind. A thought record (see appendix 2) can be used to assist you in this task. By using a thought record, one can learn to notice times when one's mood changes and one experiences strong unpleasant emotions such as sadness, anxiety, guilt or anger. Negative mood shifts, or changes in our mood for the worse, can be used as cues or signals indicating that negative thoughts have gone through our mind and negatively influence our feelings or emotions.

Cognitive therapy can help individuals to identify whether sad mood is normal, or at least understandable, or if a sad mood might be a first sign that your depression is coming back. Once you are able to identify your patterns of negative thinking, as discussed in chapter 6, the next step is to look objectively at these negative automatic thoughts. Here it is helpful to test out the validity of your negative thinking and examine it objectively. Asking yourself specific questions such as 'Am I making any thinking errors?', 'What is the evidence for and against this thought?', 'What are the advantages and disadvantages of this way of thinking?' and 'What alternative views are there?' Can be very helpful. Questioning the validity of negative thoughts can be a powerful method for discovering the extent to which one's thinking is realistic or not.

The final step in challenging negative thinking is to learn to respond to it with alternative, more helpful thoughts. By using all the information and ideas that you gather in answering the above questions, you can think of an alternative, more balanced response to a specific problematic situation. It is important to remember that many negative thoughts take the form of predictions about what might happen in the future. As we have seen in chapter 6, until you test out your negative thoughts in the real world, you cannot know whether your negative thoughts or the alternative thoughts are accurate. Therefore, behavioural experiments can be designed to test out specific negative thoughts and predictions.

Identifying and questioning the validity of our thinking, especially negative thinking patterns, in any situation that arises will help you to stop or slow down the process before it continues for longer periods of time thereby worsening your mood. This is perhaps one of the most useful skills that can be learnt to maintain a realistic and objective mood and to avoid spiralling negative moods that can give rise to another episode of clinical depression. An important advantage of cognitive therapy is that it provides prophylactic properties. That is, cognitive therapy actually teaches individuals specific strategies and techniques that they can use on a day-to-day basis for a significant period of time after therapy has ended to ensure they stay well. By learning to become your own effective therapist, you will be better equipped to prevent the return of future depressions.

## Staying well by continuing to relate well and develop healthy relationships

As we saw in chapter 8, difficult relationships and interactions with others, including friends, family, intimate partners and colleagues, can contribute to the experience of depression. We also noted in chapter 8 that relationships and depression are linked in two fundamental ways. First, depression can impact on relationships that the individual with depression has with a number of people. Second, interpersonal relationships can affect, and often contribute to, the experience of depression. In chapter 8, we reviewed an effective psychological treatment for depression called IPT, which has been shown to be as effective as anti-depressant medication and appears to lead to improvements in symptoms of depression by positively impacting on issues relating to interpersonal relationships. By focusing on key interpersonal problem areas, or the specific interpersonal context of depression, IPT can assist individuals with depression in overcoming symptoms of depression. Moreover, IPT can also help to construct healthy relationships so that you continue to relate well interpersonally in a way that further protects you from relapse or recurrence of depression. Improving the nature of relationships, for instance, by making relationships better and stronger, can help reduce depression symptoms.

Bieling and Antony have adapted some of the strategies used in IPT to help individuals protect themselves from relapse and recurrence of depression.[2] They suggest that to make changes to your relationships, it is useful to find a specific relationship issue that has affected you during your depression or that has developed as a result of your depression. In chapter 8, we noted that in IPT it is important to find the interpersonal problem area. From the perspective of relapse and recurrence prevention, it may be most helpful for the individual with depression or past depression to take a look at the description of an area which they believe has been most affected by their depression (i.e. grief, interpersonal role disputes, role transitions, or interpersonal sensitivity). This should help to identify the specific interpersonal relationship issues that need to be addressed and strengthened.

It is important to maintain an active focus on addressing relationships and making them thrive and become stronger. An important goal is to build equally positive and reciprocal relationships with people in your life. By building new, healthy and stronger relationships, you will be maximizing your social and emotional support network. Here are some specific strategies and techniques for the different interpersonal areas to help you prevent relapse and recurrence. In terms of grief, it helps to try to counterbalance the view of the relationship with the dead person over time. As we saw in chapter 8, writing down the things that were good about the relationship and those that were not so good or were bad can help develop a more balanced and less idealized view of the relationship you had with the person you lost. In this way, your understanding of what the relationship meant to you will help you to be in a better place to understand how to move forward. In terms of interpersonal role disputes, it is helpful to remember that, like all negotiations around role disputes, not everyone gets exactly what they want. However, when both people obtain at least some of their expectations, the conflict can be reduced. Therefore, over time negotiating successfully in role disputes can assist in reducing tension and conflict as well as frustrations in interpersonal relationships. In terms of role transitions, what helps here is to focus attention and your efforts on difficulties that result from role transitions, and implement strategies to reduce the negative consequences and maximize this transition in order to help you to decrease the likelihood of experiencing negative unpleasant emotions. Finally, in terms of interpersonal sensitivity, because of the nature of this interpersonal problem area, we believe that it would be more helpful and appropriate to consult with an IPT therapist in order to develop and improve interpersonal sensitivity since books may be insufficient in assisting you to address these complex issues. Often, individuals may not be clear exactly which interpersonal behaviours or areas are contributing to their difficulties in their relationship. Therefore, a professional opinion can be very helpful.

## Staying well by continuing to challenge and test unhelpful assumptions

As discussed earlier, in addition to identifying and challenging negative automatic thoughts during your everyday activities, it is often important to understand and question unhelpful assumptions, as we noted in chapter 7. Unhelpful assumptions can give rise to negative automatic thoughts in depression and can put individuals at risk of relapse or recurrence of depression. In order to change one's unhelpful assumptions using cognitive therapy, it is important first to identify the assumption and then challenge and test its validity. It is helpful to ask yourself important questions such as: 'Does this kind of belief make sense for me?', 'Is it a fair rule?', 'Would I suggest to people I love that they should adopt this rule in order to improve their lives?' If the answer to any of these questions is no, then this may be a rule or assumption you want to change.

We also discussed in chapter 8 that particular themes related to unhelpful assumptions are common in individuals with depression. These themes tend to reflect two key types of personality styles that appear to increase the likelihood of suffering from depression and the return of depression. The main two types of personality styles are perfectionism and dependency. Perfectionism appears to put individuals at risk of depression because having expectations that are too high and too strict increases the likelihood of being disappointed. Dependency on the other hand seems to increase the risk of depression because it makes individuals rely too much on others, hence preventing themselves from developing appropriate and effective skills to cope and look after themselves. It is beyond the scope of this book to describe in detail these two types of personality styles and provide specific techniques and strategies that can be used to reduce perfectionism and dependency. However, we believe that continuing to question and challenge the validity of unhelpful assumptions, and particularly develop behavioural experiments to test out the validity of these assumptions, can help reduce the likelihood of these personality styles increasing the chances of a relapse or recurrence of depression. The further reading section for this chapter provides interested readers with key information about reducing perfectionism and dependency.

## Staying well by practising mindfulness meditation

Mindfulness-based cognitive therapy (MBCT) is one of the first interventions that has been specifically designed to help people stay well. MBCT has been found to reduce the risk of relapse and recurrence in individuals who have previously been depressed.[4] Unlike maintenance psychotherapies, which tend to be continuations of CBT or IPT, MBCT has been designed as a new treatment for prevention of depression. 'Mindfulness means paying attention in a particular way: on purpose, in the present moment, and non-judgementally.'[5] Mindfulness meditation is thought to contribute to the process of challenging negative thinking in a different way. It is argued that by learning to pay attention to and accept what is going through your mind in a non-judgemental way can help weaken negative thinking patterns and shift attention to simple things. Moreover, it is thought that mindfulness meditation can make individuals more aware of changes in their thinking, which in turn can provide them with cues or signals to take more appropriate action. Mindfulness meditation has also been found to allow individuals to focus on healthy and useful things that they are engaging with, rather than focusing their attention and efforts on events or situations over which they have little control.

The first study carried out to test the effectiveness of MBCT showed that for individuals who have three or more past episodes of depression, the risk of relapse or recurrence over a sixty-week period was reduced from sixty-six per cent in the treatment as usual to thirty-three per cent in the mindfulness meditation group. This is clearly a large reduction in risk. However, it is important to note that mindfulness appeared to work better in individuals who have more risk of becoming depressed again. It is beyond the scope of this book to provide a detailed description of mindfulness meditation and MBCT. The further reading section lists books that can give a comprehensive description of what MBCT entails.

## Staying well by solving problems effectively

Stress and problems can contribute to the experience of depression. Therefore, being able to detect and solve problems before they become overwhelming may help to prevent relapse and recurrence of depression. Problem solving is an effective coping strategy for depression that involves a set of skills that can be used to address several day-to-day problems.[6]

The problem solving process can be broken into several helpful steps. These steps are presented in appendix 4. The first step involves identifying, defining and understanding the problem in clear and specific terms. For example, Claire had a history of recurrent depressions and was recently made redundant at work. She was aware that this problem could have led to another episode of depression and used the problem solving process to help her prevent a recurrence of depression. She saw the problem as not having a job to generate income over the next three months to pay all her bills. The second step involves selecting a realistic and measurable goal given the specific problem. Claire's goal was to apply for at least two jobs per week so that she could find one within three months. The third step involves generating as many pragmatic solutions as possible to achieve the goal for the problem. Here it is useful to be as open-minded and creative as possible in brainstorming possible solutions. Claire was able to list a number of solutions including: visiting all the job centres in her city; contacting friends and colleagues and asking for their help; sending her updated CV to as many companies as possible; asking neighbours about any job opportunities, etc. The fourth step involves carefully considering the advantages, disadvantages and feasibility or usefulness of each solution generated, and the likely consequences of implementing each solution. The feasibility and usefulness of each solution can be rated on a 0–10 scale where 0 is least feasible or useful and 10 is most feasible or useful. The solutions that should take priority would be those with the highest ratings of feasibility or usefulness, most advantages and least disadvantages. Following step 4, Claire's top two initial solutions to be implemented were visiting all the job centres in her city and sending her updated CV to as many companies as possible. The fifth step requires the implementation of best possible solutions in terms of their feasibility, advantages and lack of disadvantages, and planning to overcome or anticipate any potential obstacles or problems during this process. Claire anticipated that the costs of travel would be an important problem in visiting all the job centres in her city. Therefore, she planned to visit job centres located within the same areas, and to rely on friends and family for some transportation. The sixth step involves careful evaluation of the outcome or results of implementing solutions to problems in relation to the goal. If the goal has been achieved, then it would be reasonable to assume that the solution has worked and the problem no longer exists. Claire was able to find a job within five weeks of starting the problem solving process. If the solution has not worked, then it is helpful to return to step 4 and select the next best solution generated and consider whether the solution was implemented for long enough or frequently enough, whether there were any obstacles or problems that were difficult to address, or whether there are some skills that need to be attained to achieve the goal. Problem solving can help individuals with previous and current depressions to exert more control over their lives and cope with stress and problems in a way that can provide effective protection against future depressions.

## Key points covered in this chapter

- For a significant number of people, depression is a recurrent problem that threatens to return even after they have recovered from it.
- Once individuals are able to start to feel well and recover from depression, a crucial goal is to ensure that they stay well.
- A number of factors can determine whether or not individuals are likely to experience a relapse or recurrence of depression so the key to preventing the return of depression is to understand and address these factors.
- Several strategies and techniques have been found to effectively reduce the likelihood of relapse and recurrence of depression including: continuing to take maintenance medication; continuing to have 'booster' sessions of maintenance psychotherapy; remaining behaviourally active and healthy; continuing to challenge negative thinking; and continuing to relate well and develop healthy relationships.
- Other strategies that can be used to prevent the return of depression include: continuing to challenge unhelpful assumptions as well as personality styles; practising mindfulness meditation; and solving problems effectively.
- Before implementing methods designed to prevent the return of depression, it is important to ensure that the individual is free from depression for a specified period of time.

# Brief concluding remarks

When we were invited to write *Coping with Depression*, we were very honoured at the prospect of using our clinical and research experience to contribute to ongoing efforts to help understand and combat this common and devastating problem. However, given that there are several excellent books on depression, rather than just writing about what we, as healthcare professionals, believe should be clinically and academically written about depression and its treatments, we wanted to be closely guided by individuals who were or had been suffering from depression and those involved in their care. Therefore, we facilitated several depression focus groups, where individuals had the opportunity to participate in discussions and express what they believed was best or most helpful for them. We also closely consulted with their carers/families and numerous healthcare professionals. As a result, we set out to write a book about what was considered to be most helpful for individuals with depression and what the National Institute for Health and Clinical Excellence (NICE) currently recommends as best practice for clinical depression. Although there have been several recent developments in the understanding and treatment of depression, these new approaches have not yet been clearly demonstrated to be more effective, or at least equally effective, as currently recommended treatments. Therefore, we have refrained from discussing this information in much detail in this book but we have provided key references in some chapters for the interested reader. In addition, we have refrained from extensive reviews of theories and research because we were not encouraged to do so during our focus groups and consultations. Again, we have provided key references in relevant chapters for the interested reader. On completion of this book, we asked for comments from individuals who had participated in focus groups and consultations, and this feedback helped us to further revise and improve the contents so that, collectively, it served the purpose of assisting in presenting what is best for *Coping with Depression*.

Throughout the book, we have attempted to help readers understand what depression is, what its critical facts and figures are, and how it can best be treated, be it psychologically, pharmacologically or both. As mentioned previously, because we believe that there is no one treatment that might be particularly effective for all individuals or all types of depression, it is important to remember that individuals can cope with and overcome their clinical depression by changing their biology (medication), how they behave (behavioural activation), what they think and their unhelpful assumptions (cognitive therapy) and how they relate (interpersonal psychotherapy). Once individuals begin to feel well and recover from depression, it is crucial that they learn to stay well by preventing depression from coming back.

In the end, our intention is for anyone suffering from depression to fully benefit from effective treatments much like the anonymous author of chapter 1 did, because a multitude of other individuals can achieve this recovery and long-term well-being and improved quality of life. We very much hope that the strategies, methods, and techniques described in this book go some way in helping individuals recover from their depression and remain well in the future. However, it is important to remember that this book will not replace professional help from a qualified and experienced psychiatrist, clinical psychologist, therapist or your doctor. Therefore, we urge you not to bear the burden of depression alone and begin to seek appropriate professional help to assist you in your endeavours to feel well again and reclaim your life.

# Notes

## Chapter 2

### Further reading

Cooper, P. J. 2009. *Overcoming Bulimia Nervosa and Binge-Eating.* London: Robinson.

Crozier, W. R. and Alden, L. E. 2009. *Coping with Shyness and Social Phobia: A Guide to Understanding and Overcoming Social Anxiety.* Oxford: Oneworld Publications.

Freeman, C. 2009. *Overcoming Anorexia Nervosa.* London: Robinson.

Herbert, C. and Wetmore, A. 2001. *Overcoming Traumatic Stress.* London: Robinson.

Kennerley, H. 1997. *Overcoming Anxiety.* London: Robinson.

Silove, D. and Manicavasagar, V. 2009. *Overcoming Panic and Agoraphobia.* London: Robinson.

### References

1. American Psychiatric Association (APA). 2000. *Diagnostic and Statistical Manual of the Mental Disorders* (4th edn.-Text Revision) (DSM-IV-TR). Washington, DC: APA.

2. World Health Organization (WHO). 1993. *The ICD-10 Classification of Mental and Behavioural Disorders. Diagnostic Criteria for Research.* Geneva: WHO.

# Chapter 3

## Further reading

Gotlib, I. and Hammen, C. 2002. *Handbook of Depression.* New York: Guilford Press.

Hammen, C. and Watkins, E. 2008. *Depression* (2nd edn). Hove, UK: Psychology Press.

Papageorgiou, C. and Wells, A. 2004. *Depressive Rumination: Nature, Theory and Treatment.* Chichester, UK: Wiley.

## References

1. Kessler, R. C., Berglund, P., Demler, O., Jin, R., Koretz, D., Merikangas, K. R., Rush, A. J., Walters, E. E. and Wang, P. S. 2003. The epidemiology of major depressive disorder. Results from the National Comorbidity Survey Replication (NCS-R). *Journal of the American Medical Association,* 289, 3095–3105.
2. ESEMeD/MHEDEA 2000 Investigators. 2004. Prevalence of mental disorders in Europe: Results from the European Study of the Epidemiology of Mental Disorders (ESEMeD) project. *Acta Psychiatrica Scandinavica,* 109, 21–27.
3. Hammen, C. and Watkins, E. 2008. *Depression* (2nd edn). Hove, UK: Psychology Press.
4. Weiss, E. L., Longhurst, J. G. and Mazure, C. M. 1999. Childhood sexual abuse as a risk factor for depression in women: psychosocial and neurobiological correlates. *American Journal of Psychiatry,* 156, 816–828.
5. Brown, G. W. and Moran, P. M. 1997. Single mothers, poverty and depression. *Psychological Medicine,* 27, 21–33.
6. Maciejewski, P. K., Prigerson, H. H. and Mazure, C. M. 2001. Sex differences in event-related risk for major depression. *Psychological Medicine,* 31, 593–604.

7. Nolen-Hoeksema, S., Larson, J. and Grayson, C. 1999. Explaining the gender difference in depression. *Journal of Personality and Social Psychology*, 77, 1061–1072.

8. Feingold, A. 1994. Gender differences in personality: a meta-analysis. *Psychological Bulletin*, 116, 429–456.

9. Kessler, R. C. and McLcod, J. D. 1984. Sex differences in vulnerability to undesirable life events. *American Sociological Review*, 49, 620–631.

10. Helgeson, V. 1994. Relation of agency and communion to well being: evidence and potential explanations. *Psychological Bulletin*, 116, 412–428.

11. Nolen-Hoeksema, S. 1991. Responses to depression and their effects on the duration of depressive episodes. *Journal of Abnormal Psychology*, 4, 569–582.

12. Papageorgiou, C. and Wells, A. 2004. *Depressive Rumination: Nature, Theory and Treatment.* Chichester, UK: Wiley.

13. Simon, G. E., Von Korff, M., Picvinelli, M., Fullerton, C. and Ormel, J. 1999. An international study of the relation between somatic symptoms and depression. *New England Journal of Medicine*, 341, 1329–1335.

14. Andrade, L., Caraveo-Anduaga, J. J., Berglund, P., Bijl, R. V., De Graaf, R., Vollebergh, W., Dragomirecka, E., Kohn, R., Keller, M., Kessler, R. C., Kawakami, N., Kilic, C., Offord, D., Ustun, T. B. and Wittchen, H. U. 2003. The epidemiology of major depressive episodes: results from the International Consortium of Psychiatric Epidemiology (ICPE) Surveys. *International Journal of Methods in Psychiatric Research*, 12, 3–21.

15. Depue, R. A. and Monroe, S. M. 1986. Conceptualization and measurement of human disorder and life stress research: the problem of chronic disturbance. *Psychological Bulletin*, 99, 36–51.

16. Judd, L. L., Akiskal, H. S., Maser, J. D., Zeller, P. J., Endicott, J., Coryell, W., Paulus, M. P., Kunovac, J. L., Leon, A. C., Mueller, T. I., Rice, J. A. and Keller, M. B. 1998. A prospective 12-year study of subsyndromal and syndromal depressive symptoms in unipolar major depressive disorders. *Archives of General Psychiatry*, 55, 694–700.

17. Judd, L. L. 1997. The clinical course of unipolar major depressive disorders. *Archives of General Psychiatry,* 54, 989–991.
18. Solomon, D. A., Keller, M. B., Leon, A. C., Mueller, T. I., Lavori, P. W., Shea, M. T., Coryell, W., Warshaw, M., Turvey, C., Maser, J. D. and Endicott, J. 2000. Multiple recurrences of major depressive disorder. *American Journal of Psychiatry,* 157, 229–233.
19. Kessler, R. C., Foster, C. L., Saunders, W. B. and Stang, P. E. 1995. Social consequences of psychiatric disorders: I. Educational attainment. *American Journal of Psychiatry,* 152, 1026–1032.
20. Lovejoy, C. M., Graczyk, P. A., O'Hare, E. and Neuman, G. 2000. Maternal depression and parenting behaviour: a meta-analytic review. *Clinical Psychology Review,* 20, 561–592.
21. Lopez, A. D., Mathers, C. D., Ezzati, M., Jamison, D. T. and Murray, C. J. 2006. *Global Burden of Disease and Risk Factors.* Washington, DC: The World Bank and Oxford University Press.
22. Pokorny, A. D. 1968. Myths about suicide. In H. L. P. Resnik (ed.) *Suicidal Behaviors.* Boston: Little Brown.

## Chapter 4

### References

1. Greden, J. F. 2000. Antidepressant maintenance medications. In U. Halbreich and S. A. Montgomery (eds). *Pharmacotherapy for Mood, Anxiety, and Cognitive Disorders.* Washington, DC: American Psychiatric Press.

## Chapter 5

### Further reading

Addis, M. E. and Martell, C. R. 2004. *Overcoming Depression One Step at a Time: The New Behavioral Activation Approach to Getting Your Life Back.* Oakland, CA: New Harbinger Publications.
Burns, D. (1999). *Feeling Good: The New Mood Therapy.* New York: Avon Books.

## References

1. Kanter, J. W., Busch, A. M. and Rusch, L. C. 2009. *Behavioural Activation.* Hove, UK: Routledge.
2. Lewinsohn, P. M. 1974. A behavioral approach to depression. In R. J. Friedman and M. M. Katz (eds) *The Psychology of Depression: Contemporary Theory and Research.* New York: Wiley, pp. 157–185.
3. Seligman, M. E. P. 1975. *Helplessness: On Depression, Development and Death.* San Francisco: W. H. Freeman.
4. Addis, M. E. and Martell. C. R. 2004. *Overcoming Depression One Step at a Time: The New Behavioral Activation Approach to Getting Your Life Back.* Oakland, CA: New Harbinger.
5. Papageorgiou, C. and Wells, A. 2004. *Depressive Rumination: Nature, Theory and Treatment.* Chichester, UK: Wiley.
6. Nolen-Hoeksema, S. 1991. Responses to depression and their effects on the duration of depressive episodes. *Journal of Abnormal Psychology,* 4, 569–582.

## Chapter 6

### Further reading

Burns, D. 1999. *Feeling Good: The New Mood Therapy.* New York: Avon Books.
Gilbert, P. 2000. *Overcoming Depression: A Self-help Guide Using Cognitive Behavioural Techniques.* Revised edition. London: Robinson.
Greenberger, D. and Padesky, C. 1995. *Mind Over Mood: Changing How You Feel by Changing the Way You Think.* New York: The Guilford Press.
Papageorgiou, C. and Wells, A. 2004. *Depressive Rumination: Nature, Theory and Treatment.* Chichester, UK: Wiley.

### References

1. Beck, A. T. 1976. *Cognitive Therapy and the Emotional Disorders.* New York: International University Press.

2. Beck, A. T., Rush, A., Shaw, B. and Emery, G. 1979. *Cognitive Therapy of Depression*. New York: Guilford Press.
3. Greenberger, D. and Padesky, C. 1995. *Mind Over Mood: Changing How You Feel by Changing the Way You Think*. New York: Guilford Press.
4. Burns, D. 1999. *Feeling Good: The New Mood Therapy*. New York: Avon Books.
5. Wells, A. 2008. *Metacognitive Therapy for Anxiety and Depression*. London: Guilford Press.
6. Hayes, S. C., Strosahl, K. D. and Wilson, K. G. 2004. *Acceptance and Commitment Therapy*. London: Guilford Press.
7. Papageorgiou, C. and Wells, A. 2004. *Depressive Rumination: Nature, Theory and Treatment*. Chichester, UK: Wiley.

## Chapter 7

### Further reading

Burns, D. 1999. *Feeling Good: The New Mood Therapy*. New York: Avon Books.
Gilbert, P. 2000. *Overcoming Depression: A Self-help Guide Using Cognitive Behavioural Techniques*. Revised edn. London: Robinson.

### References

1. Beck, A. T., Rush, A., Shaw, B. and Emery, G. 1979. *Cognitive Therapy of Depression*. New York: Guilford Press.
2. Beck, A. T. 1976. *Cognitive Therapy and the Emotional Disorders*. New York: International University Press.
3. Weissman, A. N. and Beck, A. T. 1978. *Development and Validation of the Dysfunctional Attitude Scale*. Paper presented at the annual meeting of the Association for the Advancement of Behaviour Therapy, Chicago, USA.
4. Burns, D. 1999. *Feeling Good: The New Mood Therapy*. New York: Avon Books.
5. Fennell, M. 1989. Depression. In K. Hawton, P. M. Salkovskis,

J. Kirk and D. M. Clark, *Cognitive Behaviour Therapy for Psychiatric Problems: A Practical Guide.* Oxford: Oxford Medical Publications.

## Chapter 8

### Further reading

Weissman, M. M. 1995. *Mastering Depression through Interpersonal Psychotherapy: Patient Workbook.* Oxford: Oxford University Press.

### References

1. Klerman, G. L., Weissman, M. M., Rounsaville, B. J. and Chevron, E. 1984. *Interpersonal Psychotherapy of Depression.* New York: Basic Books.
2. Weissman, M. M. 1995. *Mastering Depression through Interpersonal Psychotherapy: Patient Workbook.* Oxford: Oxford University Press.
3. Weissman, M. M., Markowitz, J. C. and Klerman, G. L. 2000. *Comprehensive Guide to Interpersonal Psychotherapy.* New York: Basic Books.

## Chapter 9

### Further reading

Antony, M. M. and Swinson, R. P. 1998. *When Perfect Isn't Good Enough: Strategies for Coping with Perfectionism.* Oakland, CA: New Harbinger Publications.

Bieling, P. J. and Antony, M. M. 2003. *Ending the Depression Cycle: A Step-by-step Guide for Preventing Relapse.* Oakland, CA: New Harbinger Publications.

Kabat-Zinn, J. 1990. *Full Catastrophe Living: Using the Wisdom of Your Body and Mind to Face Stress, Pain, and Illness.* New York: Dell Publishing.

Kabat-Zinn, J. 1994. *Wherever You Go, There You Are: Mindfulness Meditation in Everyday Life.* New York: Hyperion.

## References

1. Judd, L. L. 1997. The clinical course of unipolar major depressive disorders. *Archives of General Psychiatry*, 54, 989–991.
2. Bieling, P. J. and Antony, M. M. 2003. *Ending the Depression Cycle: A Step-by-step Guide for Preventing Relapse*. Oakland, CA: New Harbinger Publications.
3. Greden, J. F. 2000. Antidepressant maintenance medications. In U. Halbreich and S. A. Montgomery (eds) *Pharmacotherapy for Mood, Anxiety, and Cognitive Disorders*. Washington, DC: American Psychiatric Press.
4. Segal, Z. V., Williams, J. M. G. and Teasdale, J. D. 2002. *Mindfulness-based Cognitive Therapy for Depression: A New Approach to Preventing Relapse*. New York: The Guilford Press.
5. Kabat-Zinn, J. 1994. *Wherever You Go, There You Are: Mindfulness Meditation in Everyday Life*. New York: Hyperion.
6. D'Zurilla, T. J. and Goldfried, M. R. 1971. Problem-solving and behaviour modification. *Journal of Abnormal Psychology*, 78, 107–126.

# Appendix 1: Activity chart

| | Monday | Tuesday | Wednesday | Thursday | Friday | Saturday | Sunday |
|---|---|---|---|---|---|---|---|
| 7am–8am | | | | | | | |
| 8am–9am | | | | | | | |
| 9am–10am | | | | | | | |
| 10am–11am | | | | | | | |
| 11am–12pm | | | | | | | |
| 12pm–1pm | | | | | | | |
| 1pm–2pm | | | | | | | |
| 2pm–3pm | | | | | | | |
| 3pm–4pm | | | | | | | |
| 4pm–5pm | | | | | | | |

| | 5pm–6pm | 6pm–7pm | 7pm–8pm | 8pm–9pm | 9pm–10pm | 10pm–11pm | 11pm–bed |
|---|---|---|---|---|---|---|---|
| | | | | | | | |
| | | | | | | | |
| | | | | | | | |
| | | | | | | | |
| | | | | | | | |
| | | | | | | | |

# Appendix 2: Thought record

| Date and time | Situation | Emotions (0–100) | Automatic thoughts | Alternative thoughts | Re-rate emotions |
|---|---|---|---|---|---|
| Monday 8pm | English class | Depressed (70) | I'm never going to be able to do all the work for this class. The other people here are much cleverer than me. The teacher must be wondering why I am here. | I won't know whether or not I can do it unless I give myself a chance. I can ask the teacher for help if I am finding it difficult. | Depressed (45) |

| Date and time | Situation | Emotions (0–100) | Automatic thoughts | Alternative thoughts | Re-rate emotions |
|---|---|---|---|---|---|
| Wednesday 8.30am | On way to work when I realized I'd left a report at home. | Frustrated (90) Low (60) | I'm such an idiot. I'm always making mistakes like this. This is going to ruin my day because I'll have to go back home to get the report and then I'll be late for work. | This is the first time I've left a report at home since starting this job. One mistake doesn't make me an idiot. It's frustrating to be delayed by having to go back for it but it won't necessarily ruin my whole day. | Frustrated (60) Low (30) |

| Date and time | Situation | Emotions (0–100) | Automatic thoughts | Alternative thoughts | Re-rate emotions |
|---|---|---|---|---|---|
| | | | | | |

# Appendix 3: Downward arrow technique

Negative automatic thought:

↓

What would this mean to you?

↓

If that was true, what would it mean to you?

↓

Supposing that was true, what would it mean to you?

↓

If that was true, what would it mean to you?

↓

Key unhelpful assumption:

# Appendix 4: Problem solving steps

**STEP 1:** *Identify, define and understand the problem in clear and specific terms*

_____

_____

**STEP 2:** *Select a realistic and measurable goal for specific problem*

_____

_____

**STEP 3:** *Generate several pragmatic, open-minded and creative solutions*

_____

_____

_____

_____

_____

_____

_____

_____

**STEP 4:** *Assess feasibility/usefulness, advantages, and disadvantages of solutions*

_____

_____

_____

_____

_____

_____

_____

_____

**STEP 5:** *Implement best solutions and overcome possible obstacles*

_____

_____

_____

_____

**STEP 6:** *Evaluate the outcome or results of solution implementation*

_____

_____

# Appendix 5: Useful website addresses

**Australia and New Zealand**

Australian Association for Cognitive and Behaviour Therapy

www.aacbt.org

Australian Psychological Society

www.psychology.org.au

Beyond Blue

www.beyondblue.org.au

Depression and Bipolar Support Alliance

www.dbsalliance.org

Mental Health Foundation of New Zealand

www.mentalhealth.org.nz

Royal Australian and New Zealand College of Psychiatrists

www.ranzcp.org

## United Kingdom

Association for Post-Natal Illness

www.apni.org

British Association for Behavioural and Cognitive Psychotherapies

www.babcp.com

British Psychological Society

www.bps.org.uk

Depression Alliance

www.depressionalliance.org

National Association for Mental Health

www.mind.org.uk

Royal College of Psychiatrists

www.rcpsych.ac.uk

Seasonal Affective Disorder Association

www.sada.org.uk

UK Interpersonal Psychotherapy Special Interest Group

www.iptuk.org

## United States of America and Canada

Academy of Cognitive Therapy

www.academyofct.org

American Psychiatric Association

www.psych.org

American Psychological Association

www.apa.org

Association for Behavioral and Cognitive Therapies

www.abct.org

Canadian Mental Health Association

www.cmha.ca

Canadian Psychiatric Association

www.cpa-apc.org

Canadian Psychological Association

www.cpa.ca

Depression and Bipolar Support Alliance

www.ndmda.org

International Association for Cognitive Psychotherapy

www.the-iacp.com

International Society for Interpersonal Psychotherapy

www.interpersonalpsychotherapy.org

National Alliance for the Mentally Ill

www.nami.org

National Foundation for Depressive Illness

www.depression.org

# Further Reading

Addis, M. & Martell. C. 2004. *Overcoming depression one step at a time: The new behavioural activation approach to getting your life back.* Oakland, CA: New Harbinger Publications.

Antony, M. M. & Swinson, R. P. 1998. *When perfect isn't good enough: Strategies for coping with perfectionism.* Oakland, CA: New Harbinger Publications.

Beck, A. T. 1976. *Cognitive therapy and the emotional disorders.* New York: International University Press.

Bieling, P. J. & Antony, M. M. 2003. *Ending the depression cycle: A step-by-step guide for preventing relapse.* Oakland, CA: New Harbinger Publications.

Burns, D. 1999. *Feeling good: The new mood therapy.* New York: Avon Books.

Fennell, M. 1999. *Overcoming low self-esteem: A self-help guide using cognitive behavioural techniques.* London: Robinson.

Gilbert, P. 2000. *Overcoming depression: A self-help guide using cognitive behavioural techniques.* Revised Edition. London: Robinson.

Gotlib, I. & Hammen, C. 2002. *Handbook of depression.* New York: Guilford Press.

Greenberger, D. & Padesky, C. 1995. *Mind over mood: Changing how you feel by changing the way you think.* New York: Guilford Press.

Hammen, C. & Watkins, E. 2008. *Depression* (2nd edn.). Hove, UK: Psychology Press.

Kabat-Zinn, J. 1990. *Full catastrophe living: Using the wisdom of your body and mind to face stress, pain, and illness.* New York: Dell Publishing.

Kabat-Zinn, J. 1994. *Wherever you go, there you are: Mindfulness meditation in everyday life.* New York: Hyperion.

Klerman, G. L., Weissman, M. M., Rounsaville, B. J. & Chevron, E. 1984. *Interpersonal psychotherapy of depression.* New York: Basic Books.

Papageorgiou, C. & Wells, A. 2004. *Depressive rumination: Nature, theory and treatment.* Chichester, UK: Wiley.

Weissman, M. M. 1995. *Mastering depression through interpersonal psychotherapy: Patient workbook.* Oxford: Oxford University Press.

Williams, M., Teasdale, J., Segal, Z. & Kabat-Zinn, J. 2007. *The mindful way through depression: Freeing yourself from chronic unhappiness.* New York: Guilford Press.

Young, J. & Klosko, J. 1993. *Reinventing your life.* New York: Plume.

# Index